YOU'LL BE MY SON JOE

A Story of Courage and Circumstance

With a forward by Doctor Essam A. Awad
Professor of Medicine, University of Minnesota

---

to Denny

[signature]

By
Yazdan Bakhsh

Cover art: Rick Kastenbauer
Cover and text layout: Rick Kastenbauer
Editors: Eva Ng, Connie Feil

Published by Yazdan Bakhsh, Saint Paul, Minnesota USA

ISBN 978-1-4675-2828-3 Soft Cover

Library of Congress - Pending

First Edition

Printed and bound in the United States of America

COMMENTS

<u>You'll Be My Son Joe</u> is a gripping account of an adventurous life filled with ethnic customs, innocence, growing pains, survival instincts, profound courage, and little known historical facts including that of a famous civil war. Ride along with Yazdan Bakhsh as he brings you through the lows of his misfortunes and celebrates the elation of life's lucky breaks. He imparts culture and information rarely known in the Western world. This is a must read as his message will spread like wildfire!

~ Eva Ng, President, Capital City Business Council, former Saint Paul Mayoral Candidate, CEO and Turn-around Specialist for Small Businesses and Fortune 100 Companies

Yazdan Bakhsh is a neighbor who I have been privileged to know over the past few years. We are both proud of our American backgrounds and share our belief in the American dream. My father came from Croatia when he was fourteen years old, married my mother and worked in the iron mines of Minnesota. Then the packing plants in South Saint Paul. But as a leader of his ethnic group became a city councilman, and was able to help his three children through college educations (a teacher, a nurse and a physician). As I have aged it has became apparent that many people have very interesting stories to tell, and when I read about "Joe's" story it enhanced my belief. In my conversations with Joe, I had no idea about his difficult background, it has made me more proud of his accomplishments and I wish him well with his book.

~ Anton Spraitz, Doctor of Oncology

Yazdan Bakhsh understands better than anyone, the tremendous opportunities this country gives to hard working entrepreneurial people. His incredibly uplifting positive spirit makes him a joy to be with and an inspiration. He knows the importance of working hard and also of being politically active in order to preserve the freedoms many of us might take for granted. It is an honor to call him my friend.

~ Debra Newman, President of Newman Long Term Care, and Chair for Life & Health Insurance Foundation for Education

I am very interested in reading your book! I share your love of our country and the opportunities that it permits. One of the worries I have is that our education system has abandoned its roll in turning out citizens who truly understand why our country is a magnet for those in the world, who wish to improve and control their own futures. As part of this, so many of *our* citizens are ignorant of the problems other people in the rest of the world face. That is why I feel it is so important for U.S. citizens to hear the stories of emigrant citizens who have come through such travails as yours.

~ *Scott McKee, Ophthalmologist*

One can't know Afghanistan, without knowing at least a bit about the "cultural areas" of that nation. Yazdan Bakhsh was born into the lowest group within Afghanistan's cultural caste system – the Hazara. Years later in this remarkable autobiography, Yazdan has written of the tribulations his family suffered generations upon generations. Yazdan's personal story begins with hard work. Eventually he uses his innate entrepreneurial skills to elevate himself from the system he was born into. With his good nature and inborn talents, he is incorporated into an American family working abroad. Thus forms a lifelong "family" attachment that moves to America. Here young Yazdan from Afghanistan's most discriminated culture succeeds in the immigrant's dream, to live in America.

On the one hand, this is a tale of the opportunities America has to offer. It is also, however, a tale of how difficult it is for our nation to have any impact on nations like Afghanistan, where we make enemies when even we perceive our involvement an act of outreach.

~ *Jane Pejsa, Award Winning Midwest Author*

Since the September 2001 invasion of Afghanistan by the United States, news media have kept this conflict before our eyes. Many people, however, have only a minimal understanding of this conflict and its historical background. You'll be my Son Joe is a short but very powerful account of one man's life-changing experience detailing his escape from Afghanistan and his new life in the United States. While Joe's story is a personal one, it gives the reader a short but concise history of Afghanistan while Joe shares his very personal experience. It is an excellent resource, and easy reading that will help any reader to come to a fuller understanding of the continuing conflict in Afghanistan.

Yazdan (Joe) Bakhsh arrived in the United States in November 1975 with a tourist visa. Shortly afterward his American mother enrolled him in Archbishop Grace High School in Minneapolis, where I met him. Yazdan graduated from Archbishop Grace (now Totino-Grace High School) in 1978 while I was Principal.

The information is remarkable and the way in which Yazdan has woven in his personal story makes it very interesting, yet easy to read.

~ *Brother Milton Barker, Assistant to the President*
Totino-Grace High School, Minneapolis, Minnesota

DEDICATION

I dedicate this book to two people that have always given of themselves, and who changed my life. They gave me hope and opportunity, which ultimately gave me peace and success in the greatest of nations. I am privileged to call Dr. Charles and Mary Louise Simkins my American father and mother.

I also dedicate this writing to my children. May they always live in freedom and enjoy the opportunities that freedom offers.

In Afghanistan
"If we worked we ate, if we didn't work we died"

CONTENTS

FOREWORD

If you are one of the millions of people who wonder why the United States is in Afghanistan, and you are having difficulty understanding the current problems in that part of the world, you will find many answers to your questions in this book.

The author was born in a small village in Afghanistan, lived there (if one can call this living) and suffered unbelievable existence in that strange society. He was under the rule of different war lords and later on the Taliban. He describes in details what his people were like and makes the reader feel that he is there among them.

He tells in honest narrative how he escaped to Lebanon and eventually got a job as a guard to an American family, who later on adopted him, and made it possible for him to realize his dream of coming to the United States. There he continued his education, enjoyed freedom and became a successful entrepreneur.

The book is concise, easy to read and contains a plethora of information about life in Afghanistan. I strongly recommend it to everyone interested in the real truth about the current situation in that part of Asia.

ESSAM A. AWAD MD, PhD.
Professor of Medicine, University of Minnesota

INTRODUCTION

MY HOMELAND

It began almost two millennia ago with the death of Muhammad. Two separate ideologies developed in the Muslim religion. One group called Sunni, believed that going forward they should choose a strong religious follower to be their next earthly leader. The other sect, the Shi'a believed that a descendant of Muhammad himself should carry on this leadership. The two ideologies became separated forever.

Afghanistan is where my story begins. Afghanistan is located in southwest Asia, northwest of Pakistan, and east of Iran. Land locked and roughly comparable to the state of Texas in size, it shares its longest border with Pakistan. Afghanistan's maximum length from east to west is about 770 miles, from north to south it is about 630 miles. Its climate is arid to semiarid with cold winters and hot summers. Temperatures can vary greatly during a single day. Most of the country is covered by rugged mountains with plains in the north and southwest. One half of Afghanistan averages over 6,000 feet in elevation. The highest peak, located near Afghanistan's northeast border is over 24,000 feet. The plains to its north are dry and treeless steppes, and its southwestern corner is desert.

The Hindu Kush Mountains, which go from northeast to the southwest, divide the northern provinces from the rest of Afghanistan. Its capital and largest city is Kabul. About eighty percent of the population is engaged in agriculture. Arable land is only twelve percent of its total land area. Over eighty percent of the population lives in rural areas. Of those living in urban locations, almost half live in Kabul. The population of Afghanistan in the year 2000 was estimated at over twenty five million.[1] But that population has changed with the ongoing conflicts and migration out of Afghanistan due to the political climate.

There are five dominant languages in Afghanistan with Farsi

3

being one of them. In Afghanistan approximately one-fifth of the population call themselves Hazara. The name is thought to have come from the Persian word for thousand, *hazar*, referring to a military unit of one thousand soldiers. The Hazara are the most persecuted people in Afghanistan. The Pashtuns, which comprise over forty percent of the population, are the dominant group in Afghanistan. Eighty percent of the Afghanistan population is Sunni Muslim, the Shi'a make up only nineteen percent.

Pashtuns are Sunni Muslims while Hazara are Shi'a. The Pashtuns have discriminated against the Hazara people for generations. Even though freedom of religion is written into the Afghan constitution, it is poorly adhered to. Abuses occur on a regular basis from the predominate religion. The government is run by Pashtuns. Therefore children of Hazara descent are born into servitude in Afghanistan, where they have been subjugated for hundreds of years, a carryover from tribal conflicts and wars.

The Hazara have been inhabitants of Hazarajat, a mountainous region in central Afghanistan since around the second century. The Hazara people of Afghanistan have physical features resembling the descendents of Mongolian Chinese, but are believed to also have a mixture of Persian and Turkish ethnicity.

Afghanistan green area shows Hazarajat
Source: *Joshua Project / Global Mapping International*

4

It is believed there is a direct history of Hazara relationship to Genghis Khan the Mongolian conqueror. In the thirteenth century, Genghis Khan conquered the inhabitants of central Afghanistan. It is said that his soldiers settled and intermarried with the local inhabitants. The Mongolian soldiers who settled among the Hazara contributed to their culture. Many Hazara tribes and family names have been taken from names of distinguished soldiers, and from Mongol feudal lords. There are many Mongol terms still used by the Hazara in their language today. As evidence of this historic relationship it is not uncommon to hear parents tell their children to sit up straight like a Mongol, or to work hard like a Mongol.

Hazarajat, the land of the Hazara people in the central highlands of Afghanistan, was historically ruled by tribal chiefs, war lords, and dynasties in a feudal fashion. Hazarajat's invisible boundaries have changed throughout history based on occupation, conquerors, and civil and political unrest. The Tajik peoples were also early inhabitants to the area and have lived in close proximity to the Hazara. They may have been a contributing influence to the Hazara culture to accept farming and raising livestock as a settled life, and the acceptance of the Farsi language.

In the Bamian Province of Afghanistan there were huge Buddhas one hundred eighty feet tall carved into the mountain side. The Buddhas have been the historic guardians overseeing the Bamian valley for over fifteen hundred years, but in 2001 they were destroyed by the Taliban when they came into power. The Buddhas were considered by the Taliban as non-Islamic idols, there was no respect for their historic significance. It took the Taliban many days using explosives and firing rockets at the giant Buddhas to destroy them.

The Hazara have always been regarded as honest, faithful, open, and hard working. They readily seek opportunity and value education. It is what has set them apart most from the Pashtun and *Kuchi*. It is ironic, but one Pashtun ruler insisted on having only Hazara as his personal guards.

Growing up Hazara meant servitude even for the very young;

as they were considered inferior by the Pashtun. The Pashtun utilized their privileged position in society as oppressors to the Hazara, a status they have enjoyed for generations. The Pashtun people consider the Hazara people lower than animals. The Pashtun regarded the Hazara to be even beneath that of the historically detested Jews and the Christians.

Because of generational suppression by the Pashtuns, the self chosen ruling elite, the Hazara were relegated to doing the least desirable jobs even in their own mountainous region of central Afghanistan. To this day, they are preyed upon by the Kuchi, an annually migrating people of Pashtun descent.

Most Americans know little about Afghanistan and its people, especially the Hazara. Americans understand little about the culture of the Islam religion, and have had minimal exposure to people from that part of the world. Increased immigration from those nations to the United States is changing our awareness. Opinions of most Americans are formed by what is presented on televised media. Reports of terrorism, Islamic extremism, bombings, and the deaths of our American servicemen fill the airwaves. There are no reports about the plight of the Hazara, their struggles, nor their persecution.

The traditional Hazara homeland, Hazarajat, is a mix of steep mountains with high peaks, often hidden by clouds. It is a place of rugged terrain and deep valleys and bold beauty, as though a giant paint brush tinted the landscape. But, for those who have to live there, it is a barbarous, challenging existence. The small scattered plateaus throughout the land are where the subsistent Hazara farmers grow their grain.

The Hazara have experienced eras of what we now call genocide. As I mentioned, they have been suppressed and discriminated against for centuries by the Pashtuns, which control the government. In the 1890s, three significant wars occurred where thousands of Hazara were killed and put into slavery by the Pashtun King Abdur Rahman. They were disarmed, their villages sacked, leaders imprisoned or executed, and their best lands were given to Kuchi nomads. Afghanistan's history has been plagued with ruling ethnic warlords and unrest.

The wars devastated their population, and kept the Hazara in subservience. Before the genocide the Hazara were the largest ethnic group with over sixty percent of the population of Afghanistan. The wars reduced their population by fifty percent. The Hazara have been discriminated against by all subsequent rulers, which has kept them in the highlands.

The genocidal wars against the Hazara forced them from the fertile lowlands to the rugged highlands. Although repressed in Hazarajat, their mountainous homeland, the harsh environment has given the industrious Hazara the fortitude to endure and survive.

Life did not improve for the Hazara when the Taliban came to power. The Taliban would gather groups of Hazaras and shoot them en masse in a public display.

This was the way of life I remember in Afghanistan, one child born into servitude and disregard, the other into well being and opportunity.

Hazaras judged by King Abdur Rahman 1890s

Afghanistan has had a tumultuous history. From 1747 to 1973 Afghanistan was a Monarchy. In 1973 the king was overthrown, and Afghanistan was proclaimed a republic. The Russians invaded in 1979. In 1992 a series of civil wars divided Afghanistan. In 1996 Kabul fell to the Taliban, and the American presence began in 2001. (See Appendix for History of Afghanistan)

[1]Http://afghanistans/Information/People/Population.htm

CHAPTER ONE

GOD'S GIFT

It was a cold, two room dwelling that was my home. I lived with my mother and father, sisters and brothers. Our house was one of many built in a row attached end to end. Each housing unit was divided into two large rooms. One room was where the family lived and the other was for the livestock. We shared a common wall between our animals and ourselves. As you walked into our house a door opened to where we lived, then next to it was an open entrance where we kept our sheep, goats, chickens, cows, a horse and donkey for hauling and transportation, and a bull. This arrangement kept the livestock close and safe, and added to the overall warmth of the structure in the winter.

In the village of my childhood, there were no more than forty homes arranged in three long rows. Our home was located in the shortest row. This way a wall was shared between each dwelling, an efficient and energy saving way to build. The only stand alone house was that of the Mullah, and the mosque which was centrally located. The mosque was the hub of activity, especially during the winter. In the mosque boys would study reading and math, and the Koran. Many mosques at this time were kept warm during winter with a fire burning beneath its stone floor. The stone became heated and dissipated the heat throughout the building. The mosque was usually busy with activity.

Buildings were made of sand, clay, and straw with flat roofs of the same material built over a wood frame. At times we had to patch the roof, especially in winter. In the center of the roof a hole allowed the smoke of the fire from the *tandoor* to escape. The tandoor was a large cylindrical shaped clay oven, dug into the floor of the home in which meals and bread were prepared. The fire burning in the tandoor imparted a characteristic smell of burning manure intertwined with the smell of bread and meat juices, to create its own unique blend.

The tandoor is an efficient oven used to prepare food with its hot air convection heat used for cooking and baking, especially for flat bread called *nhan*, a common staple. Bread was made in the tandoor oven by patting it against the inside of the clay structure where the radiant heat would bake it. Meats and vegetables could be skewered and laid over the top of the oven to cook. It is the same today as when I was a child, homes still commonly use a tandoor to cook meals.

Pots were also placed atop the tandoor for cooking. The tandoor would heat the ground around it and a cover was placed on top to keep the heat in. At night the family would sleep around the tandoor under warm wool blankets made from the sheared coats of our sheep. If the family was large, a clay pot with coals in it could be set in an open area and a blanket placed over it to keep the heat in. Five or six children could easily sleep around the warm pot. This was called a *sundalee* (a generic term for table).

The rows of houses are usually built near a spring or water source. Our village had a small natural flowing *chashma*, spring, used for drinking and cooking. But we had to walk about ten minutes to a larger water source for our livestock to drink. We carried water by hand in clay jugs and animal skins to our dwelling and utilized our pack animals to transport larger clay vessels of water. In our daily chores and activities we used clay pots for storage, cooking, and carrying water. There was usually someone in the village, or in a nearby village that made pottery from clay. Drinking water was kept cool in large clay vessels. A particular clay pot suited for use with yogurt was called *quza*. People would also carry items on their heads.

In the short growing season of the high mountains we grew wheat, barley, peas, potatoes, onions, and carrots. We also collected wild plants. Many foods would be dried and stored for the winter. We had bread every day but not always vegetables. Other times meals would consist of eggs, yogurt, whatever vegetables or fruits were available, *quroot* made from milk, and nhan, flat bread. If we had meat it would usually be chicken, sheep, or goat. It was less common to have beef, unless a cow or bull died of old age or was sick. We never let anything go to waste. If a cow was butchered it would usually be shared with others in the village. We also had a horse used for transportation, and a bull for working. Even with harsh winters, we had to be sure to maintain our chickens and livestock so they could breed.

Our village was a community. We relied on each other to share our resources and work together on projects that benefitted the community. For example, a village may support an animal driven water wheel. Or, several families would go together to share the costs of sponsoring such a device, and then charge a small fee for other villagers to use. Similarly as I mentioned, when one family butchered a large animal like a cow they would share with others. This assured that each family got a portion of the meat, and that there was no waste because no refrigeration existed.

During the spring and summer, villagers would gather their goats and sheep together to be herded to higher plateaus to graze. This was a community event and each family took turns watching over the livestock. When the livestock was brought back to the village at the end of the day to milk and bed down, all the individual sheep and goats knew which houses to go to. It was almost comical to watch them split up and go in their own separate directions to the families that owned them. The next day would be a repeat.

To separate seeds from the wheat shafts we piled shocks of cut wheat in a circle. A horse or donkey would be led in a continuous circle, while dragging a bundle of shocks and sticks tied together, over the pile of wheat. The process separated the seeds from the shafts. When finished, a portion at a time would be taken from the pile and thrown in the air with a pitch fork to separate the shafts from the wheat. Without steadily prompting the animal to perform this duty, it would stop its chore and eat the wheat. Many times this was done at night when it was cooler for the animal. This was one of my duties as a child, to ride on the back of the animal doing this task. My job was to make sure the animal kept moving so the process would not stop. One time riding on the back of a horse, I was so sleepy going in a continuous circle, I fell off.

Most families had a hand grinding wheel. Operating this as a child would often times make my hands chafe and bleed. It was a grinder that consisted of two stones a little over a foot wide. The top stone had a hole in its center where the wheat was poured, and a handle to rotate it. By rotating the top stone the wheat was ground and the resultant flour came out from between the stones. This was a necessary but arduous job. My sister would help me. We were both very young and did not have the full strength to operate it by ourselves. I would turn the wheel by its handle, a half turn to where my sister could reach it. She in turn would rotate the handle back to me to complete a continuous cycle. Together we were able to continue this shared duty to produce enough flour to make nhan.

Each family in the village had livestock. Many nights wolves would come out, and because our livestock shared the same building the wolves would sometimes jump onto the roof over our livestock and try to dig through the roof. There were also large domestic dogs in the village, one time I remember the wolves subdued and ate one of the village dogs.

According to my passport, I was born a Hazara in 1956 in one of the provinces of Afghanistan called Orozghan. My family spoke Farsi, one of the more common languages in Afghanistan. I was told that my name means "God's Gift" in Persian. Many believe there is something in a name; mine has brought me luck, life, and a new beginning. My ultimate freedom has been God's Gift.

It is unknown why Orozghan province is listed on my passport as my birthplace. It is a distance from Kabul and at the fringe of our traditional mountain homeland of Hazarajat. My family may have been in that province when I was born. After my birth, before I can remember, my family must have gone to Kabul for its opportunities, and then to our Hazara homeland in central Afghanistan. There is where I remember my earliest days. I believe to this day that I was actually born in Kabul.

Hazara family names were usually developed from geographic locations, or from names of important past heroes or rulers.

Because of the decades that have passed, and the fact I was working and living away from my family beginning at a young age, I never asked questions of my father or siblings about our family history. I use my name given to me when I was born, not a family surname, which I do not know. My father's first name was Hussein. My name may have been given in honor of a famous Hazara in the Bamian area one hundred years earlier, Mir Yazdan Bakhsh, an influential Hazara chief that controlled the passes into Bamian. (See Appendix, History of Afghanistan)

It is a practice of the government to register male Hazara children as two years older than their natural age. They do this so the Hazara males can be inducted into the military sooner. Persons from the Afghan government would make the journey annually into Hazarajat to register new births. The officials would automatically add two years to their age, unless they were paid *bakhsheesh,* a willing gift or bribe. Many of these villages were only accessible by horse or on foot.

Hazara children grow up fast. That is to say, they learn at an early age their position in society. They learn quickly that their culture is subservient to the other cultures in Afghanistan. Even in their traditional land they call Hazarajat, they are not safe. Despite their poverty and low status in their own nation, the Hazara are an industrious people. This has helped them with their survival. They still remain a hopeful people. Hazara usually marry young and settle close to their childhood homes.

From the earliest age, children help with household duties. That is how I remember my earliest years. The whole family would walk from our home to the small plateaus and flat areas, large enough to plant wheat and barley, and other crops. Some of these fields were a distance from our home. The family would spend the day tilling and planting, younger children would pull weeds. Sometimes as we worked in the fields we would roast the green wheat stalks and peel open and eat the grain. I also remember as a small child when we heard thunder crack and then saw a rainbow after a rain, we would run and look for mushrooms. We thought the thunder had opened the earth and

13

allowed the mushrooms to pop out.

As I think back to my childhood in the mountains of Afghanistan, we had to work hard just to live. We had little leisure time. Things were done simply with the resources at our disposal which nature usually provided. Living with our livestock just on the other side of a common wall, fleas were a continuous menace. To rid our clothes of fleas we would hold our clothes over the heat of the tandoor and flees would let loose and drop into the fire. An elderly man in our village would pile his clothes on an ant hill so ants would eat the fleas in the clothes. He would then shake the clothes off and wear them. He was old and did not have good eyesight to see such small things.

As I have said, we did not waste anything and utilized every part of an animal. If the animal died naturally or was sick we would use it. Animal skins were especially important. They were used for storing water and liquids. Animals were carefully skinned and their skins sewn to make watertight vessels. Another use for a goat or sheep skin was in making quroot from milk. First the milk would be heated then cooled in a large clay container. The cooled milk would be separated by pouring it in an animal skin, which was hung tethered with the neck of the skin slightly angled up. It had to be continuously agitated to separate out the butter. This was another duty for children. With one child on each side, siblings would push the skin back and forth. Butter would gather at the angled area of the neck and be skimmed off.

The mixture remaining from the milk after the butter had been removed was put into a cloth bag. This removed the water which thickened the mixture to become yogurt. Some of the yogurt was kept to drink with bread at meals. The rest was thickened to become quroot which was salted and rolled into pebble sized balls and placed in the sun to dry. Most of the balls were stored for food during the winter, but also carried to the fields to eat while working. For regular meals quroot was mixed with water, stirred to liquid consistency and drank with nhan. If stored properly in an airtight vessel and kept in a cool place, quroot keeps for extended periods.

During the summer there was no time for children to play. All children were busy helping the family in the fields, taking care of the livestock, collecting wood and dried manure for winter heating and cooking, and helping with routine family chores. In the winter we still had chores to do, which also included shoveling off the roof, but children found time to play and interact. I would gather with the neighbor children, we cleared a circle in the snow and played marbles. Our marbles were made of clay, stone, and bone. We would supplement lost or broken marbles with a small round bone from a sheep, goat, or young calf's leg. We made the best of warm sunny days in the winter.

As a child in the summer I wore sandal-like footwear, or most of the time went barefoot. Before winter we would use animal hides to fashion clothes and foot wear for winter. I took care of the family livestock, during the day I would bring them to areas where they could graze. One fall day when snow was already on the ground, and I had not yet had shoes made for me for the winter, I lost control of the sheep and goats. They were hungry and ran off to forage for food. They were my responsibility, I had to gather them and bring them back to our shelter. With no shoes I froze my feet and struggled to walk for over a week.

In the harsh environment of the highlands of Afghanistan, it was important to gather everything you would need in winter during summer. All summer long families would be busy preparing for winter which could last five or six months and bring heavy snowfalls. In higher elevations of Hazarajat cooler temperatures begin toward the end of September with snowfall in October. Afghanistan overall is a dry and arid area, and the higher the elevation the cooler and more inhospitable it becomes. In the spring the ice capped mountains would melt, causing runoff. This could be devastating in those years that had a lot of snow. Summers were short and warm.

I remember before the cold weather would come, I would go to the highest mountain so I was closer to god, to pray that the coming winter would not be so harsh. Before the winter had ended we were usually short on food and would go two to three

15

days without eating. As a child I was always hungry. With the lack of fresh fruit in our diet, and limited quantity of vegetables during the long winters, we were susceptible to vitamin deficiency. One of my cousins developed an eye disorder because of this. During the winter I would sometimes sit in the warm sunlight, not knowing at the time that it was helping my body absorb vitamin D.

On occasion we would travel to nearby villages over coarse and narrow paths, which became impossible during the winter. As a child I remember routes to other villages were nothing more than camel or horse paths. When the Russians came into Afghanistan they made rudimentary roads through some of these areas. This made it possible and easier to travel to other areas and villages, but also made it easier for our traditional enemy, the Kuchi to come to our villages.

Afghanistan has been a traditional crossroads for trade since historic times. These traders used one of many mountain passes, most of them thousands of feet at their high points. One famous pass is the narrow Khyber Pass that has connected Afghanistan and Pakistan through the northeast part of the Spin Ghar mountains. This range forms a natural barrier between Pakistan and Afghanistan; therefore the border between the two countries runs along their summits, which reaches heights of 15,000 feet. Historically, the thirty three mile long Khyber Pass was part of the Silk Road. It has been an important trade route between central Asia and south Asia. One of the highest points along the Khyber Pass is 3,500 feet.

Many invasions of the area have come through the Khyber Pass. Ancient conquerors as Cyrus II (Cyrus the Great) and Darius I, both Persians of the Achaemenid Empire, Alexander the Great, and Genghis Khan are known to have come by way of the Khyber Pass. A soldier in the last British invasion of Afghanistan in 1919 stated, "Every stone in the Khyber [Pass] has been soaked in blood." This has been the historic significance of the Khyber Pass. After World War One the British built a railway through the pass. It continues as an important route for transportation of food, supplies, and people even today.

As a child in Hazarajat, I remember we would feed our livestock in the morning and then go about our daily chores. One thing I remember collecting to burn in the fire, and to stockpile for winter, was a small bush that grew only about two feet high. We would use a hoe like tool to uproot it, and then pull it out of the ground and store it to dry. *Boutah* is the general word in Farsi for a small bush. In back of our house is where all our supplies to get us through the winter would be piled. There was hay for the livestock, dried manure and boutah bushes that we had collected to burn, and piles of other materials.

Our fields were divided among families in the village. Each family would till, cut weeds, and harvest their plots. We would carry the wheat back to our village on donkeys. There, the women and children would separate the sheaf by hand. The sheaf was separated by throwing it into the air. Hazara women work very hard. Their days are long and never ending.

Because trees are not very plentiful in the mountainous area where my people live, we would collect dried manure to burn. We would collect and carry it in large woven baskets on our backs. These baskets would be made during the winter. As a child this was one of my duties. I was so small that the basket kept slipping to one side as I would pick up dried animal droppings. At times I lost my struggle with the basket, and it would fall off my back spilling its contents. One time I got so upset with the manure falling out that I set the basket down and kicked it, which only caused me an explanation and a repair when I returned home. Once baskets were filled, they were dumped against the back of our house. We also worked the fresh droppings from our livestock into a size and shape that was most suitable for burning in the tandoor.

Another duty I helped with was the salting and hanging of strips of sheep or goat in the fall to dry for winter use.

As I mentioned I remember always being hungry as a small child. One day when my parents went to the mosque to pray I was left with my siblings in our home. I was so hungry that I ate

17

from the yogurt my stepmother was preparing. When my father found out he punished me. As he scolded me he asked, "which hand?" I was scared that he was going to cut my hand off. He punished me so hard that it hurt me to walk for several days. This reinforced a strong cultural reminder that we all eat and share together. That is how we have endured for millennia.

One time I remember as a small child I worked for a prominent Hazara family with a lot of land. I do not think I was more than six years old, but worked in the fall for about a month helping to gather wood and help the family with any chores a small boy could do. Even though my day was from before sunrise to after sunset, I liked working for the family because they fed me. I earned my food. I remember many days when I came back with the family from the fields I was so tired that I could hardly walk anymore. I was concerned however, because I had to sleep outside, and constantly worried about wolves eating me. There were others working for the family including adults that also slept outside. I was comforted to wake during the night and see the others.

I was quite young when my mother died in childbirth. In a one room *khana*, house, there was little privacy. All functions within the one room were known by all, and space was coveted. I must have only been five years old but I remember my mother lying in pain during labor. I sat leaning against a post feeling the anguish in the room. I felt helpless and knew this was serious, I sensed it. But as a small child what can you do? You can only look on, be silent, and hope. It is a great trauma to a child to lose a parent. A child is defenseless and must rely on others. I remained frozen as I watched.

I remember that she gasped loudly, and there was no more life in her body. I was told she had died. This is the only memory I have of my natural mother. Even though I was very young, because of its tragedy this childhood experience is locked permanently in my memory.

There were no doctors and comforts for my people in Hazarajat. As a child growing up in the mountains of Afghanistan I never knew that there were such things as doctors and nurses.

As a child I only had one set of clothes. I only received a new set of clothing about once a year. By that time the previous set was ragged and torn. I do not have photos of me or my family from my youngest years. I did not know what a camera was, we did not even have a mirror so I did not know what I looked like, or did I know there was such a thing as television. All these things I discovered when we moved to Kabul. We lived at a subsistent level. I would always pray that there would be more food the next day, especially during the winter.

As I have mentioned, most of my remembrances of Hazarajat are from my childhood. Because of my young age, many of my memories are vague from those early childhood years growing up in the mountains of Afghanistan. Some things that occurred at the time I did not understand, but learned early when to be cautious and when to run and hide. I knew as a child not to ask questions. I had two sisters and two brothers, and step brothers and sisters, and two step mothers while I was growing up.

After the death of my natural mother, my father married a woman who had two children. She came to our household with her children. One day while we sat outside enjoying the warm winter sun, I learned from her children that they had lost their father and a brother to the Kuchi, leaving their mother a widow. My step mother always saw to the needs of her own children before us, especially with chores and meals. She only remained a year with my father in our household. One day while my father was gone she packed her few belongings and left with her children. She walked to the neighboring village where her parents lived.

When my father returned to discover that she was gone, he went after her. When my father met up with her and her children they were halfway to her parent's house. My father beat her and accompanied her to her parents' house, which disgraced her further. Women had few options at that time in Afghanistan. Their duties were many and their days were long, everything had to be done by hand.

19

Less than a year later, my father took another wife. This time a young woman with no children came to our house. It is customary to pay a dowry to the father of a daughter you choose as a wife. My father had to pay a sizeable dowry for my second stepmother. She was from a better family and had never been married. My father gave sheep, goats, and cows, over thirty livestock as payment for her. This left few livestock and only one cow for us. My siblings and I were concerned that we would not be left with enough livestock to have for food and use. As I have mentioned, we were always hungry as children because there was never enough food to fill us up. We relied on our livestock for our existence and survival. They supplied us with milk, meat, eggs, wool, skins, and did our hauling and plowing. They were also our means of transportation.

My new step mother and my father had a son. She always gave her child first choice of things and catered to his needs before ours. She would only feed us after her son had been cared for, we would receive a piece of bread and maybe some yogurt. My siblings and I were afraid to say anything to my father or step mother. If we did not follow her every wish she would let our father know and he would take disciplinary action. He always reinforced her. There was no win or negotiation with my stepmother.

I always had a strained relationship with my father. He was a strict disciplinarian, and followed the long tradition of demanding respect from his children. As children we would have to stand when my father entered the room. When he had guests they would eat first and we were not allowed to interact, or even to look at them. I never really got to know my father, that is, his beliefs and philosophies, and his background. I knew he was a demanding and a self-centered person. He would always eat first and receive the best and largest portions. Raised the way I was, I knew as a child you did not ask questions. You were expected to go about your day and do your chores. Everyone had to contribute and each of us had chores and family duties to do.

My father must have struggled most of his life. He was a

subsistence farmer in the mountains of Hazarajat when I was a child. After moving his family to Kabul he eked out a living by repairing shoes, setting up on various streets in Kabul. It seemed that much of his later life was concerned with the Kuchi perusing him. That is why we ultimately settled in Kabul with its large population. A relative told me once that when my father was younger he was known for having a good voice, and was handsome and tall.

As a child I remember that my father had a gun that he would hunt small game with and shoot at wolves. He had to keep the gun hidden because either the Kuchi or the government would take it away. There were very few guns in our village.

I knew, already at a young age, that Afghanistan had no future for me.

CHAPTER TWO

THE KUCHI

The Kuchi are Pashtun nomads who, for centuries, have traded between Afghanistan and Pakistan. They spend the winter season in Pakistan where it is warmer, then caravan into Afghanistan. The name itself implies "nomad" or "migration." Traditionally they are nomadic herders and therefore bring with them sheep, goats, and other livestock and carry their belongings on camels in search for grazing lands. They trade animals and a variety of goods obtained in one area to sell in another area, and trade products from their livestock for wheat and vegetables, and other necessities. These nomads have connected Afghanistan to other Middle East areas and nations for centuries.

Throughout history this activity has brought an exchange of goods through annual trade. The Kuchi follow an ancient migration from the mountains of Afghanistan to the Indus Valley in Pakistan, a fertile area where many early civilizations began. They weather the winters in the milder climate of the Indus basin. Because they are Pashtuns they have traditionally been looked upon favorably by Afghan rulers and kings, who are themselves Pashtuns, and therefore the Kuchi are allowed to do their annual migrations. During the writing of this book, many Kuchi were still seasonally migrating by traditional camel caravans. Some have modernized and now use trucks and motorcycles.

Since the Kuchis were Pashtuns, they treated the Hazara peoples the same as did the rest of the Pashtun population, with insolence and arrogance. When the Kuchis would come into a Hazara settlement, they would graze their animals in Hazara fields. The Kuchi would also leave their cows for others to tend until their return the following year. They would setup tents to live in during their travels. The Hazara are fearful of the Kuchis since they do what they want with Hazara land, property, and people. The Kuchis are allowed guns, and the border patrol is sympathetic to their annual migrations and allows them to cross the borders even in times of political unrest. The Hazara consider the Kuchi as outlaws that are allowed to do as they wish.

The government gave the Kuchi permission to trade into the highlands of Afghanistan, but the Kuchi abused the privilege and took advantage of it to subjugate the peoples of the highlands, especially the Hazara. If the Hazara did not pay them for a contrived debt, like when the Kuchi forced my father to take material to sell for them, they would take their livestock or children. They would shoot the Hazara if they dared to tell the authorities about the abuses. The Kuchi would also play tricks on the Hazara. They would bring a paper and say that certain land belongs to them. Because many Hazara at the time were unable to read, the Hazara could only comply with it, besides they dare not refuse. The government is still unable to control the actions of the Kuchi. And since the Kuchi threaten the local populations, many atrocities go unreported.

Hostilities have continued to the Hazara to the present. The American invasion of Afghanistan after September 11, 2001 against the Taliban, relieved their persecution under the Taliban, and gave them a reprieve to pursue their livelihood and lives. Concern is that once the Americans leave Afghanistan, the malicious traditions will return and continue to hold the Hazara oppressed. Many Kuchi were brought into service by the Taliban when they came into power, and were the Taliban's main supporters.

The Taliban would say that if the Kuchi killed a Shi'a they would go to heaven. The Taliban would stop a car at random or at a checkpoint, and if the occupants were Shi'a they would kill them. They are ruthless to the Hazara. The Taliban say it is OK to kill Hazara because they do not consider them as real Muslims.

There is a belief among the Kuchi that they are the oldest group in Afghanistan, and are originally from northern Afghanistan but with repeated invasions were displaced to the south, and to their migration lifestyle. Both groups have historically existed in the area for quite some time but as to who was first is uncertain.

As a child in the highlands of Afghanistan, I remember the Kuchi would come into our village and take over. They were vicious and you could not say or do anything, or they would shoot you. The Kuchi would come like gangsters and give us demands. They usually came in large enough numbers and all carried rifles so that if we rebelled they had enough firepower to subdue us. They also threatened us not to tell the authorities. There was no policing in the area.

An incident occurred just before the writing of this book. In 2011 armed Kuchis looted and burned twenty-six villages and killed five persons. Reportedly over a hundred Kuchi with guns ambushed the villages at night. These Kuchi attacks still occur every year during the summer months with their annual migration. In many of the remote areas where the Hazara live and the Kuchi migrate through each year, there is little law and judicial oversight. Therefore the atrocities the Kuchis commit go unreported and unpunished, leaving the Hazara to their fate. The Kuchi purchase guns in Pakistan and are seldom seen without them.

When the Kuchis came into our area, children knew to run and hide because the Kuchi would steal children. We knew they would enslave children, barter them, or work them to death. At night they would be tied up. Girls would suffer a worse fate. They would either be sold into prostitution, or kept by the male as his own concubine. Since they were nomads, it would be impossible to find a child that was taken by the Kuchi.

Sometimes boys would be kept as an adult's "play thing," to be dressed in girl's clothes and to do with them what they wished. This could occur regardless if the male member had a wife and children. The scenario was presented in the novel, *The Kite Runner* by Khaled Hosseini. (See the Appendix) Although the book is fiction, it incorporates many elements of reality in its storyline.

The Koran is specific on this kind of behavior and actions, which are strictly forbidden in Islam. It prescribes that those who do such a thing should be burned, as opposed to stoned. Growing up as I did, in fear of these Kuchi nomads and the atrocities they would inflict on our people, I had no regard for them and considered them totally barbaric. They were a disease to our people, who they have suppressed and discriminated against, like a defeated enemy, for centuries.

After tasting freedom from their control and persecution, if I had to return to that life, I would not have survived. I would sooner die at my own hand than at theirs. I vowed to myself that my fate would be different. As I have mentioned, the Kuchi consider the Hazara people to be like pack animals, to carry things from one place to another, and do the work they do not wish to do themselves. Not only the Hazara, but the other northern ethnic groups, the Tajiks, Uzbeks, and Turkmens also fear and distrust the Kuchi.

I do not point out these bad examples as a reflection on Islam, but to those who abuse it. The majority of Muslims follow the core practices and teaching of Islam to be better persons. It has been the extremists that use Islam and its preaching to gain power and be in control. This has always been the challenge of our culture with its close association with Islam into its every facet of our lives, existence, and politics. There has been little separation of what is called in the United States, of religion and politics, i.e. "church and state."

As a child of only six years old I remember a time specifically when the Kuchi, on one of their annual migrations, came to our village in Hazarajat. Children would run and hide, this time to hide I burrowed with other children into a nearby haystack. My eyes and nose would burn from the hay and dust. To this day I suffer from allergies. It is the custom for each village to have a spokesperson, like you would have a village mayor in the United States. It was usually an elder of the village, as was the case this time.

From our hiding place in the hay we saw the village elder trying to negotiate with the Kuchi, only to be struck with a rifle butt; he rolled into a ditch, injured. The Kuchi then shot a cousin of mine in the leg, and critically injured another in the neck. They did this to intimidate the people of the village. Harming my innocent cousins was their way of showing the village that they were in control. I was petrified because I could have been next.

To this day I have vivid memories of the Kuchi coming into our village with their guns always inseparably visible over their shoulders, and most of the men sporting a beard. It has been difficult for me to revisit these memories. I tell these stories to my American friends and they cannot believe that people still have to live this way in other parts of the world. Afghanistan still struggles today from its history of conquerors, war lords, civil wars, and with the occupation of American troops at the writing of this book.

During another of their annual migrations the Kuchi came to our village and visited our family. They demanded that my father take a quantity of cloth to sell, and dictated the price they expected for it, and told him that they would return for the money on their fall migration back to Pakistan. This was a forced indenture on my father and our family, and they expected the money from him. My father knew that he had no choice in the matter, so our family chose to leave and hide before the annual Kuchi migration back to Pakistan in the fall. My father knew he would not be able to obtain the quantity of money the Kuchi expected. To not have the money when they returned would put him and his family in peril.

At that time I was about seven years old and my father had me work for the Kuchi for a month during the summer. This must have been in part to appease the Kuchi, because it was the same year the Kuchi put the material in our home. I would watch their cows, took them grazing, and brought the cattle to the Kuchi women to milk. I would have to hold the young calves by the calves' mother so the cow would milk. One time, one of their Rams bunted me on my backside so hard that I fell into a muddy ditch. I remember that the Kuchi woman was nice to me. She even gave me clothes that her children had grown out of to replace my ragged clothing.

27

As I said, to escape the Kuchi during their return migration my family left our village. We traveled to other villages and towns in northern Afghanistan. One time we traveled to Mazari Sharif in Northern Afghanistan, a holy place for Hazara and Shi'a; but my sister did not return with us. I was quite young at the time and assumed she was married, which meant that my father would have received a dowry.

We ultimately settled in Kabul, where I had an uncle. We traveled to Bamian, a day's walk from our village, where we could get transportation to Kabul. My father sold our animals to buy our transportation. We rode to Kabul in a truck. Kabul had a large population and my family had relatives there. We would be safer by blending into the population of a big city. It would also give us better economic opportunities. I had just turned eight years old.

It was interesting to learn years later, from a long time friend, Dr. Sajady who had been the head of the American hospital in Afghanistan; he observed that given their lifestyle, the Kuchi had the lowest cholesterol, and least incidence of cancer and heart disease he had experienced. Even cholesterol levels in people living in Kabul were higher than those found in the Kuchi. In spite of this, because of their harsh nomadic lifestyle, life expectancy was not much over forty years of age. The Kuchi were also very illiterate.

While still a preadolescent in Kabul, I worked for and lived with a Panjshir family. I was about nine years old when my father arranged for me to work for the family. Unlike the previous families I had worked for, they let me sleep inside their home and treated me like one of the family. We even ate meals together. This was the first time as a child that I felt full at meals. They also gave me clothes. The family was kind and well educated. The father, who was retired, had worked for the government. Out of custom and respect, I referred to the patriarch of the family and his wife as you would a father and mother.

The Panjshir family had four daughters; one attended a university in the United States, and another was handicapped. I would clean, grocery shop, and run errands for them. One time they took me to a cinema and I saw a movie about Iran, it cemented my goal of eventually living in Iran. In the movie all the people were happy, they were all driving cars everywhere, and the landscape was beautiful with pleasing music. The movie was probably to promote tourism to the country or was a documentary, but it stayed in my mind. I learned that Iran had Shi'a Muslims, like me, as a predominant population.

Even at nine years old I rationalized that I would be treated better if I were surrounded by people like myself. The movie also reinforced to me that going to Iran was achievable, that it was only a few days bus ride from Kabul. After this realization, I was unsettled and longed to improve my life.

It was decades later that another Panjshir by the name of Ahmed Shah Massoud (ma–sood) became known as the "Lion of Panjshir" during the Soviet Occupation. He was an architect by trade who became a charismatic leader fighting for Afghanistan's freedom, first from the Russians and then the Taliban. He repelled the Russians nine times in the Panjshir Valley. When fighting the Taliban his forces were pushed into the Panjshir Valley in the northeast corner of Afghanistan. When the Taliban warned him that little land remained that they had not taken, Massoud threw his hat on the ground and said, "If only the land that my hat covers is left, I will fight for it."

Massoud was assassinated only two days before the September 11, 2001 attacks that occurred on the World Trade Center Towers in the United States. (See Definitions in the Appendix)

Panjshir Valley area of Afghanistan highlighted
Source: *http://en.wikipedia.org/wiki/Panjshir_Province*

When I was about eleven years old in Kabul, my aunt's husband got me a job working for a Polish woman who was employed in Afghanistan through the United Nations. I did household chores and took care of her dog. I remember that she had a lot of bottles of alcohol. I still grasped onto the dream, from the movie I had watched with the Panjshir family, of going to Iran. There I felt I would be treated better and have more opportunities. I began to save as much money as I could even though my father would come to claim my wages.

After one year the Polish woman's assignment was over, but she introduced me to a Polish man that was also living in Kabul, and he let me work for him. The Polish man worked as an engineer for the Polish government, and was sent to Afghanistan to oversee the assembly of bicycles. Bicycles are a common form of transportation in Afghanistan.

The Pashtun landlord saw me come and go to where the Polish man lived. With easy access, because he had the keys to all apartments, the landlord stole some items from the Polish man's apartment. The landlord then called the police and put the blame on me. I was immediately arrested and taken away. I had worked for the Polish man for about a year at the time.

While in jail, to keep me awake the police would poke me with a needle. Keeping me deprived of sleep was their method to push me into confessing about the theft. Being a Hazara did not help my situation.

My fate was sealed, but luck was on my side because we knew a man who was the Shah's cousin. He had rented to the Polish woman and lived next to her. The Shah's cousin regularly became inebriated, and at times would be seen in the street shouting, cursing, and waving his arms at passersby, while still in his sleeping gown. Regardless of the taboo against alcoholic spirits he spent many of his days inebriated. Alcohol is not a ready item to be obtained in an Islamic country. My uncle worked for a chef that cooked for foreigners, and the chef had access to alcohol. He was able to obtain two bottles of liquor to give to the Shah's cousin in return for a favor.

The Shah's cousin came to the jail with my brother. He was drunk, swearing, and still in his house robe. He demanded my release. Causing quite a commotion with his actions and threats, the police chief dropped to his knees and bowed his head at the feet of the Shah's cousin, pleading for his life. I was immediately released, with the threat from the Shah's cousin to all the police that I was never again to be taken. He threatened that if they ever touched me again, that he would line them all up and have them shot. His position as cousin of the Shah gave him power and status, despite his alcohol addiction.

When the Shah's cousin would be out in the street waving, cursing, and shouting, those passing by would drop their heads pretending not to see him, thereby, not having to acknowledge his behavior, and violation of the religious dictate against consuming alcoholic spirits.

The payment of favors and bribes is embedded in the culture, and as previously mentioned, is called basheesh. Thereafter, I was safe from the police.

CHAPTER THREE

MY ESCAPE; FROM SERVITUDE TO FREEDOM

When I was about fourteen years old I got a job in a small hotel with a restaurant. I would clean, serve customers, and pick up tourists and bring them to the hotel. There was competition for tourists; you had to promote your hotel over the competition. The job gave me interaction with people from around the world. I learned from them as I waited on them. I received tips for my services and was able to save money. At times my father wanted to take my money, but I refused him. I had a goal to save my money to go to Iran.

The restaurant was on a second level with shops beneath. It was a long narrow structure. At one end was a small hotel with only about five rooms and a common bathroom. I had a small station with two chairs and a small desk near the entry. I greeted people and set them up with a room or seated them in the restaurant and waited on them. A greater portion of the building was devoted to restaurant and kitchen. The entrance led to an open area where tourists could set down their baggage while they arranged for lodging. From this area one could enter the restaurant through a door, which first opened to a section separated by a curtain where the women ate, before leading into the main restaurant where men and boys ate. At the back of the restaurant was the kitchen; it was opposite a door that led down a flight of stairs to the street.

I stayed at the hotel and restaurant where I would sleep in a landing at the upper part of the stairs to the hotel and restaurant. This gave me good surveillance and I would be awakened if any lodgers tried to leave during the night without paying. This was part of my job which also gave me a place to stay. I would also bring guests to the local bus stations. The stations would give a small commission for my loyalty to keep me bringing guests to their location.

One busy lunch time, I was seating and waiting on customers, as two familiar Kuchi men appeared. A chill ran through me as I looked up at them. They were the same Kuchi that had dropped the material off expecting my father to sell it for them years earlier. They recognized me as well, as the son of the Hazara man, who they felt owed them a debt. I greeted them, took their order and brought their food. They inquired about my father and I told them I thought he was dead.

They would not leave my station and insisted on eating their food there. Not wanting to lose sight of me, they did not want me to close the door as I went into the restaurant for their food. They did not believe me when I told them that women were dining on the other side of the door. When I opened the door the Kuchi men saw all the women eating in the sectioned off area, and several women showed their displeasure about the men looking in at them.

I told the Kuchi men I had to wait on some customers and would return with drinks for them. I then hastily left out the rear door of the restaurant. I scurried down the outside stairs and ran along the walls of buildings next to the walkway. I ran for miles to the outskirts of Kabul until I found myself at the base of the mountains. I was born and partially raised in the mountains; it is ironic that I had to return to the mountains for protection. It was a narrow escape. That night I built up some rocks, and dug a hole large enough to nudge into under a large rock, to give me some protection from my childhood fear, wolves.

I did not know if the Kuchi men had learned about me working at the hotel and restaurant, or if they just chanced upon me that day. More than likely the Kuchi had intimidated the people in my village back in the mountains to learn where we had gone. That was usually how it happened.

I knew I could not return to the hotel where I worked and slept as they would continue to look for me there. So, I went to my sister's house. For the next few weeks, I stayed at different places. I did not dare stay in one place too long. Since the Kuchi knew I was in Kabul, I had to be careful where I went and what I did. The Kuchi never forget a debt, and they will search until they find you. They were intent on finding my father through me and to even the score they had with him. Even though this was a debt imposed on my father, and one that he dared not refuse, it was now my burden. If they could not find my father to settle the score, they would expect me to pay the debt.

It would do no good to go to the authorities. They would only reinforce that my family owed a debt that had not been paid. Besides, I was a Hazara, and they would not have taken my side on the issue. I knew I could not avoid the Kuchi that were looking for me, indefinitely; it was time that I pursued my goal. If I was unable to get a passport, I would find a smuggler to get me over the mountains.

After a month of avoiding the Kuchi men I was determined to get a passport. My brother worked with a man who knew a person associated with the government. He could introduce me to someone in the interior ministry so I could get a passport. I would have to pay the cost. As I have explained, the whole culture functioned on basheesh, which is paying a tip to get what you want. This time it would be *reshwat*, an imposed and expected bribe, and harder to negotiate. I had to pay a person to get the contact in the ministry; then pay a bribe to the ministry person himself for the passport.

The ministry person asked fifteen hundred rupees for a passport, but I only had one thousand rupees. My sister gave me a carpet to sell and use the money toward purchase of my passport. With my brother's help we were able to bargain to reach an agreement. At the time seventy rupees was the value of one American dollar.

I ultimately had to bribe three people to get my passport. I was advised to wear traditional clothing so I would look older, and to convince the authorities I was a poor peasant who only wanted to do a pilgrimage. They listed me as a landowner. The first picture on my passport had me wearing a traditional headdress.

As I said, I had to give a reason why I was requesting a passport. I told the authorities that I wanted to visit the holy site in Mashhad, Iran, not far across the border northwest from Afghanistan. Many Shi'a go there. It is one of the holiest cities for Shi'a Muslims. An ancient city, it was an important oasis along the historic Silk Road. The name is Arabic for martyrdom, where Imam Reza, the eighth Imam of the Shi'a Muslims is buried. Estimates of up to twenty million Shi'a visit Mashhad each year.

Once I received my passport, good for only one year, I wasted no time to travel by bus to Iran. When I left Afghanistan my intent was to never return. My visa given by the Iranian government was for about two weeks. I was only sixteen years old at the time. The only immediate employment I could find in Iran was working in the fields. I cut down wheat all day. Centered in Tehran, work crews would be bused to fields outside the city to work for the day. It was hard work, but gave me an income. Between the long days, hard work, and dusty conditions, with no protection from the mosquitoes at night, I got very sick.

Plowing in Iran as done in Afghanistan

To renew my visa I had to travel to other countries, and stay a few days so the authorities would not be suspicious that I was trying to maximize my time by going from country to country to renew my visa and therefore be able to stay longer in Iran. But that is exactly what I was doing. In Iraq I got my visa renewed to visit Iran for two months by saying that I wanted to visit more religious sights. I would repeat this process again and again for each visa renewal. Next, I travelled to Kuwait, then back to Iraq, then Syria, and Lebanon. I usually had to pay the customary bribe as well for the visa renewal. I traveled to all these countries by bus.

It also gave me an opportunity, when traveling from country to country, to sell in one country items that were not as readily available, that I had obtained from a different country where they were cheaper. I learned this merchandising from another Hazara that I had met. It gave me some extra money. I would usually bring with me some electronics to sell. For example, I purchased some items common and plentiful in Iran, to sell them in Iraq for a small profit. I learned for instance that clothes and pistachio nuts were cheaper in Iran, while radios were more expensive in Kuwait, and therefore would bring those items to the respective country when I renewed my passport. It was basic supply and demand, but I was only able to take several items across at a time. Otherwise, I would have to pay a customs duty on them. This was a common practice to gain extra money, and was still occurring when I returned to visit the area decades later.

In 1970 I arrived in Beirut, Lebanon but could not find any work so I was forced to sleep two nights in a park. Someone told me that Bekaa Valley would be a better place to find work with all its agriculture. I finally got a job in the city of Baalbek, in Bekaa Valley for a restaurant where I would clean and wash dishes. I was given a tiny room built into the owner's home, but had to use the bathroom at the restaurant.

The type of bus I rode from country to country

Unfortunately, I broke too many dishes to suit the owner and was told to look for another job. As luck and opportunity have followed me, as I waited to cross at an intersection, a Lebanese man pulled over in his car and asked if I were going somewhere. Trafficking in hashish was so prevalent that sellers were always looking for tourists to sell to. Seeing I still had my uniform on from the restaurant, he inquired if I had been working. I told him that I had just lost my job. Pondering a moment, he then asked if I would consider coming to work for him. It had been only two minutes that I was out of a job! I accepted his offer and got into the car.

The Lebanese man owned an antique store that catered to tourists. He wanted me to work just through the tourist season. My job was to make coffee in the morning and serve it to customers as they entered, and while they shopped. I would also lead the tourists around on a Camel outside to have their pictures taken. This job fit my skills. I enjoyed interacting with the customers, especially foreign tourists. My boss paid me thirty Lebanese pounds a month and gave me a place to stay complete with a shower, a luxury I had not had before.

38

Map of Lebanon from the Central Intelligence Agency
World Fact Book
Source:http://en.wikipedia.org/wiki/file:Lebanon-CIA_WFB_Map.png

I did well with people and sales. I started selling more items than my boss. Recognizing my potential, within four months my boss gave me an increase in wages to one hundred pounds. I was also given the opportunity of full time employment. To catch the attention of tourists and passersby I would stand on our camel and have it circle around the circular Roman ruin next to our store. It worked. Cabs would pull over at the request of their passengers, and tourists would stop to take photos and shop.

People would ask me questions in many different languages, especially about the prices of things. I tried to learn a little of each language, especially how to count in each language. The tourists that came into the antique store were on their way to the Baalbek ruins and I only had ten or fifteen minutes to interact and sell them something. If I talked price in their native language it took less time and I had a better opportunity to sell them something.

The antique store was only one kilometer from the main Roman ruins of Baalbek. The small Roman structure by the antique store, built about the same time as the main ruin, was somehow related to it. For bringing tourists to our store, and to assure loyalty, we gave taxi drivers a twenty percent commission on anything their tourists bought. This was good incentive and added to the stores success.

Looking from the main road is the antique store where I worked and lived, our camels are in the middle of the picture between the antique store and the Roman ruin

I had a good personal relationship with my boss and his family. I would have dinner at his mother's house one kilometer from the antique shop every evening. I liked the job and my boss, and enjoyed the interaction, but always tried to have a backup plan or opportunity in case things would change. Given the uncertainty that I grew up with and only having myself to rely on, a contingency plan always gave me peace of mind. I had my health and ambition; these had to carry me through.

My contingency plan in this case was that I also taught karate, something that I had been introduced to while still in Kabul, and which I continued to pursue while working at the antique store. I became a karate instructor teaching part time. Because of my facial features and my experience with karate, many people thought that I was Japanese. At the time also, there were popular movies that featured karate. Because many thought I

40

looked Japanese, they gave me the nickname, "Okamoto." This was the name of one of the Japanese Red Army terrorists who attacked the Tel Aviv airport in 1972. Ironically, Okamoto and his comrades had been trained in a mountain camp near Baalbek. (See Definitions in the Appendix)

A fruit and vegetable market in Beirut with vendors displaying their wares

I worked three years at the antique store. This gave me the opportunity to become familiar with peoples and languages from around the world. I enjoyed interacting with the customers and learning to speak a little of their languages, I picked up on languages quickly. My job in the antique store also gave me the opportunity to get to know many of the local police and taxi drivers.

On one routine day in 1974 a United Nations project manager from the United States came into the store. His name was Dr. Charles Simkins, from the State of Minnesota. He was to be the head of a United Nations project, with the mission to reduce and ultimately eradicate the growing and selling of hashish. To accomplish this, he hoped to convert current farmers from growing hashish to growing food crops like wheat, sunflower seeds, corn, and fruit and vegetables, instead.

In his own description Mr. Simkins describes his duties, "Our United Nations project focused on convincing the Lebanese farmers to grow sunflowers and potatoes, and other crops instead of hashish. However, the Lebanese farmers could make quick money from growing drugs, which were smuggled out of Lebanon. The American Embassy suspected that the president's son was also involved with the smugglers." That is how widespread the problem was.

The UN program was designed in cooperation with the Lebanese government. One initiative of the United Nations development project, under its Food and Agriculture Organization (FAO) was to build a plant to process sunflower oil from the seeds. The plant would buy sunflower seeds from farmers and process them into oil, and then sell the oil domestically and abroad. An infrastructure would then be setup to help guarantee the success of the program. Sunflowers were chosen because they can be grown in areas with little moisture. Hashish takes a lot of water, and there were gun battles over water rights because of the heavy need for water when growing hashish.

Part of this program was to buy hashish fields, destroy the hashish and plant food crops. Beets were another potential crop considered for the program. This initiative between the UN and the Lebanese government was being instituted as the industrialized nations were having epidemic growth in drug usage. It was hoped the program would have success and offset some of the increases in hashish growing.

Mr. Simkins asked many questions about the area and its culture. During his visits, he would inquire about crops, farming, and hashish growing in the area. It was not wise to talk openly about hashish growing, especially if you were an American. I interacted with him and tried to answer his inquiries about the area. Growing hashish was a way of life for many farmers who supplied smugglers with their product. It was lucrative for everyone involved, especially the smugglers. The smugglers did not trust outsiders and would readily protect their livelihood by whatever means necessary. Many times hashish farmers had family members involved, brothers or cousins were the smugglers for their crop.

By the third time Mr. Simkins came into the store asking troubling questions, and making comments about his program, I pulled him aside and cautioned him about asking such questions and the comments he was making. It was not safe for Mr. Simkins to openly discuss how his program would convert hashish fields to food crops, this could have got him killed.

Growing hashish and smuggling was a way of life. Occasionally, smugglers would contact me and invite me to their homes. They wanted more customers and hoped I could help them. They saw me interacting with many foreigners, and were drawn to me because I did not look Lebanese. These smugglers would have readily paid my way and expenses to Europe and other countries, in order to find new buyers. One smuggler even operated his own plane that he used to deliver his hashish.

Since the use of hashish was taboo in Islam, the consensus among those who grew the hashish and those who smuggled it was, "We sell it to you, it is your problem if you are so dumb to use it." Fellow Muslims who used the drug were considered bad and looked down upon. The nations of Turkey and Syrian were known for their harsh treatment of drug violators.

Mr. Simkins would periodically visit the antique store for coffee. Many times while riding the camel to the antique store, Mr. Simkins would pass by and wave. Our interaction and relationship began to grow. At other times he would see me on my morning run. I would sometimes run four to five miles in the morning to relieve stress and anxiety. I would run also at night to reduce tension and to sleep better. This was my way to deal with problems and concerns which were out of my control, and had to be left to fate. This I have done all my life. On many of these mornings Mr. Simkins would drive by and we would give a mutual greeting to each other. It was not long before Mr. Simkins invited me to his birthday party. From there my relationship grew with him and his family. I think Mr. Simkins was drawn to me initially because I was also a foreigner in Lebanon.

Observing how good I was at my job and how well I interacted with people, Mr. Simkins related to me years later, that he had no doubt that someday I would become a shop owner. I had always been an entrepreneur at heart. I had a desire to better my condition in life, and that is what kept me motivated. Unfortunately, the political system deteriorated, and it was not to be.

Baalbek Roman Ruins near the antique store where I worked

Looking down from the Baalbek ruins, my boss seated in the middle, is grinding coffee in a mabal, a traditional device which with its rhythmic sound also serves as a musical instrument. He is accompanied by a man on his right playing a rababa having only one string. The men are selling coffee to tourists. The small white cups on the tray were used for coffee.

Camel with calf in front of antique store and interested tourist. I stood between the calf and tourist because she was afraid of the protective new mother.

Standing on our camel circling around the Roman ruin next to the antique store, this helped attract tourists.

Since I left Afghanistan my life had changed, I was working and able to save some money, and I had many friends in a different country that had much more to offer than my homeland of Afghanistan. Now I also had a link to America through Mr. Simkins.

About this same time, Mr. Simkins was looking for a secretary for his FAO program. He wished initially to hire a Lebanese woman for the position, but the local women did not want to live in Baalbek. An American by the name of Rachel was introduced to Mr. Simkins, and was hired by him after an interview at a Beirut pub. Rachel had to be vetted thoroughly by the Drug Enforcement Administration (DEA) staff at the American embassy because she would be working with drugs.

Rachel had come to Lebanon for a three week visit to her sister in 1971. Her sister was married to a Lebanese man. Rachel came to visit and liked the area so much she decided to stay. She was able to get a job teaching English. Then she got a job with the Daily Sketch a local newspaper. Rachel was able to rent an apartment near her sister. The locals were hesitant to rent an apartment to a single woman, especially an American.

Rachel learned quickly that she had to dress properly and always be cautious, and to be careful where she went. She was also cautioned not to take a camera with her to avoid suspicion from the locals. One Lebanese women who Rachel got to know summarized it best to her, "We don't like Americans here you know." They wanted to throw them out. Another obstacle that Rachel had to deal with was her name. Her first name was Theresa, but she went by her middle name Rachel. The locals were suspicious that she may be Jewish with a name like Rachel.

After Rachel was employed by the FAO program she would accompany the two Greek engineers who also worked on the project. Whenever the three of them would go down a street together, the Greek men would keep Rachel between them for her safety. Persons working on the international project were always aware of the culture they were in. On several occasions when the Greek engineers went out, Lebanese men would try to start fights with them.

Rachel worked with a young Lebanese woman whose boyfriend made threats about Rachel. The coworker told Rachel that her boyfriend thought she was a bad influence on her, and the coworker's boy friend would tell his girlfriend that he threatened to harm Rachel. He also threatened Rachel to her face.

When Rachel was teaching, prior to working for the FOA, there was an anti-American demonstration at the Palestinian Camp near Beirut. Fearing that Rachel would become targeted, the school administrator asked her to leave the school for her own protection. The school arranged a taxi to take her back home safely.

Later, when Rachel was living in Baalbek and seeing a Lebanese doctor, an explosion occurred in a Palestinian training camp in the nearby mountains. A trainer had dropped a mine which exploded. The story that came out of this incident was that Israel had bombed the camp. This gave the Palestinians the opportunity to promote the tragedy for their own purpose.

There were constant challenges for Rachel as a single American women living in Lebanon. Once while visiting a hashish site one of the plain clothes policemen that accompanied her, picked up a handful of hashish, put it in his handkerchief and gave it to Rachel. She knew she had to get rid of the hashish because it would not be good to be seen with it.

When Mr. Simkins came to Bekaa Valley in the fall of 1974 he rented a villa in the town of Bait Chama. The villa was owned by a man who lived in Kuwait, but whose elderly father living in the nearby mountains, would visit the property daily and assumed the caretaker duties for his son. There was a vineyard in back of the house; the elderly caretaker would come each day to prune and nurture his grapes. At various times when the grapes were ripe he would bring us some.

It was a gated house on several acres of land in Bait Chama about ten miles from the village of Zahl. The Bekaa Valley area is fertile with mild winters and dry warm summers, which have limited rainfall. The valley stretches through Lebanon north into Syria. It was a good central location, with Beirut on the coast a little over fifty miles west of Bait Chama, and the border of Syria not more than a thirty minute drive to our east.

Assuming the duties of Project Manager for the Drug Abuse Control Project, under the United Nations FAO program, Mr. Simkins setup a local office in Baalbek; the headquarters of

FAO operations were in Beirut. Its mission as mentioned earlier, was to learn about the status of hashish production in the area, and find ways to convert producers back to growing traditional agricultural crops. The increase in drug usage throughout the world made harvesting cash crops such as hashish and opium, very lucrative to farmers. Converting these growers back to farm crops would be no easy matter. Making it even more difficult, was that many local farmers admitted that local politicians were getting a cut of the money hashish would bring.

Mr. Simkins even proposed a loan program, where the United Nations would borrow money to local farmers to help with their conversion. But the UN program heads were not interested. Most of the farmers were poor; Mr. Simkins thought this would make a difference for them, and for the program. With the growing drug problem throughout the world, and especially in the industrialized countries, the United Nations program was designed to address the problem at its source.

These programs in host nations were run as partnerships between the United Nations and the host nation. The nation that the UN partnered with was supposed to contribute their half of the project to maintain the program, but many times the United Nations had to fund the entire project itself to keep it going. There were other complications to managing such programs. One time Mr. Simkins had equipment that he had ordered for the project, stolen in the port of Beirut.

Mr. Simkins examines a hashish field

In Mr. Simkins own words, "There was much to learn and become accustomed to, a new culture and many people to meet; including members from both sides of the project, and the local Lebanese people." During his initial visit in 1974, Mr. Simkins stayed for about six months to set things up. He returned with his wife Mary Louise and their youngest daughter Sally, in March 1975. In April, the family along with Rachel his secretary went on a trip to Hungary. They returned April 14th, 1975 the day after the fateful violence that caused a sectarian reciprocation. They were advised by Ali, Mr. Simkin's personal driver, to stay a few days in Beirut until things settled down. They stayed about three days in the Mayflower Hotel before returning to Bait Chama.

Hashish fields were common in Bekaa Valley. In some areas where there were standing fields of hashish on both sides of the road, if you opened your windows the scent of the hashish was obvious and would even make you euphoric and dizzy. In America we call this cannabis plant by many names: Marijuana, pot, weed, and grass. Hashish means "dry weed" in Arabic and is a concentrated form of Marijuana. The sticky resin is collected from the leaves and flowers of the cannabis sativa plant, dried, and then compressed into various shapes for ease of transport and use. In Lebanon they rated the quality of their hashish crop by one, two, or three, with one being the highest quality.

Newly planted hashish field in Lebanon

High quality hashish field ready for harvest

As I have mentioned, my relationship with Mr. Simkins continued to grow through his stops at the antique store, by our ongoing interactions, and visiting his home. By September 1974 I asked Mr. Simkins if there would be a possibility to work for him.

Unfortunately, because of my non Lebanese citizenship status, I could not work in his program. But, that same month, on the suggestion of Mr. Simkins I accompanied him to the American embassy in Beirut, where he introduced me to Joe the head of the Drug Enforcement Agency (DEA) at the embassy. As a foreign national I could not have gained entrance to the embassy on my own, especially since my citizenship was still with Afghanistan. After I had been formally introduced by Mr. Simkins to Joe, thereafter, I went on my own to visit with him. The DEA was interested in the status of the production of drugs, especially the status of opium in the area.

It was rumored at the time that the Turkish were teaching the Lebanese how to grow poppies, from which they could harvest opium (the Papaver somniferum poppy). Opium has been known for its anesthetic properties since prehistoric times. The Papaver somniferum poppy has been discovered in Neolithic settlements. The plant was grown by the Sumerians who referred to it as the "joy plant." Ancient Egyptian healers instructed persons with pain to chew the seeds from the poppy to relieve their agony. It has been a cash crop for hundreds of years. The history of opium goes back many millennia and would fill volumes.

The DEA wanted to know how much influence the Turkish had in the area, and to what extent they were producing opium. Turkey has been a prime exporter of opium and has improved its growth and yield. For subsistent farmers opium was also a crucial cash crop, even though growing poppies is haram, forbidden, in Islamic Law.

As I mentioned there were rumours the Turkish were teaching local farmers how to grow poppies, and the processes involved to manufacture opium from them. It was also suspected by the DEA that the son of the Lebanese president was also involved. He would even arrive by helicopter to various sights. I was to interact with local growers and try to bring samples back to the embassy. Joe paid me in cash, American dollar bills.

Although I was still working at the antique store, this gave me

52

another opportunity to earn money. As mentioned, the growing and manufacturing of drugs was rampant in Lebanon, especially in Bekaa Valley. Even my own boss at the antique store sold hashish. I was seventeen and considered the good money more than I did my own risk. My work for the embassy DEA officially started October 1974. I received one hundred dollars the second time I visited with Joe.

I was warned by Joe to watch what I said, and for future visits not to come directly to the embassy. Instead, I was advised to walk to the embassy and shop along the way so I would not cause any suspicion. Although I only visited the embassy once in December 1974, I was very involved in my new job with Joe between January and March 1975. I was busy trying to collect samples. As I mentioned Joe wanted to know how involved the president's son was in the drug trade.

I had become friends with a Lebanese man that everyone knew was making opium. He would pick me up at times while I was jogging, and invite me to his home for dinner. The man was cooking the tar right in front of me in his home, using common kitchen cooking utensils. He asked me during one dinner if I wanted a sample. I told him that I had another person to sell it to. Always looking for other buyers, he was willing to give me a sample and a percentage on any hashish or opium I was able to sell.

The Lebanese man would "bleed" the poppies. This involved cutting the bulb to allow the tar-like fluid to ooze out overnight. The fluid was then "cooked", boiled to leach out the opium. I also knew a Turkish man, but he was not involved with opium. He would come to the antique store to milk the camel when it had a calf. The man would give me some of the camel's milk to drink. It was rich and fulfilling.

At my third visit with Joe at the embassy, I explained to him how they were making opium. The DEA head asked me if I could get a sample. I received two hundred dollars in American currency at this visit. A month later I brought a sample of opium to Joe in a small bottle, I was paid five hundred dollars for my efforts.

I only worked for the DEA at the embassy until the Simkins returned in March 1975. Learning how involved I was with the DEA, and the danger it put me in, Mr. Simkins told the DEA head that it was getting too risky for me. Instead, Mr. Simkins gave me a job working for the family. I am sure that his wife, Mary Louise also had a key role in his decision to give me a job working for the family, I started in April 1975. I would drive the Simkins, run errands, grocery shop, and guard their villa. Mr. Simkins paid me in cash.

I quit the antique store at the end of April 1975. With the growing conflicts and unrest there were fewer tourists. The business was struggling and my boss tried to keep me employed, but it was becoming a struggle for him to do so. I had a good relationship with my boss but with the reduction in tourism I knew he could not keep me employed much longer.

While living in the Bekaa Valley, Mrs. Simkins volunteered to teach English in Zahl, about ten miles away from Bait Shama. She was only able to teach for a month because of the increase in conflicts and hostilities. Mary Louise as a teacher was very nurturing, but resolute in her principles. One day in her class her students got rowdy and Mrs. Simkins told them to, "Stop teasing each other." This caused them to laugh and carry on even more, when she repeated again that they should not "tease each other" it was followed by heightened laughter. She was very upset by their actions and disrespectful behavior.

I would bring Mrs. Simkins to the school and pick her up. That day she was frustrated and in tears because she did not know what was causing the poor discipline and behavior from her students. When she explained what had happened in her class that day, I too laughed when I heard what she had told the students, and explained to her that *tiz* in Arabic refers to a person's butt. When we got back to the villa, Mrs. Simkins shared her story with the whole family, and we all laughed together.

Most houses in the area had a fence or wall built around their yards. The Simkins house was set on about two acres, and had a brick wall around it. Built on top the wall was an additional wrought iron fence with sharp points that rose up from the wall. This gave it added height. In the back of the villa was a grape vineyard. The Simkins also had a horse they kept in the back acreage. Someone had given Mr. Simkins the horse and it was named *Harb*, war. We all rode the horse. One time while riding the horse I was shot at. Not sure where the shot came from I wasted no time getting out of the immediate area.

In late June 1975, the two Simkins daughters Joann and Jane, came to visit and stayed until the end of August. They were able to celebrate my birthday in mid July. Jane had just finished high school for the year in America, and Mrs. Simkins thought it would be a good opportunity to spend some time together. As parents, having their daughters with them helped resolve any worries they might have had about two young women on their own for the summer, half way around the world.

Mr. Simkin's driver Ali picked the two girls up at the airport, at one point during their trip to Bekaa Valley Ali cautioned them to duck down for their safety. Although the two daughters were happy to reunite with their parents and younger sister, they missed the autonomy they would have had on their own for the summer, back in the United States.

During their eight week stay they traveled around the area. Having parents in international service, both daughters had lived in the Middle East before, and were aware of the cultural differences. They knew to keep themselves as low key as possible, especially since they were women. They traveled and shopped, they enjoyed the custom of being able to taste things before you purchased them.

Jane enjoyed sunning herself in the back yard so she had a dark tan, which was set off by her blond hair and blue eyes. One time while shopping, an Arab woman behind her shouted and then lifted the back of Jane's blouse enough to scratch her with a fingernail. Jane was shocked, but this is not an uncommon occurrence in the Middle East. Jane was wearing a top popular at the time that had short sleeves and rode high enough to show the belly. The local woman must have been surprised by Jane's dark tan but light hair and eyes, and therefore decided to investigate.

Another time during the daughter's stay, Jane was sweeping the veranda when a car with four Arab men with masks and guns jumped the iron fence. Jane dropped the broom and ran into the house. Her mom pushed her and her sister into a closet and told them not to come out no matter what happened. The girls heard a lot of dickering and then shots go off, and then it got quiet. Scared and not sure what to do next, they were relieved when their mother opened the door and told them they could come out. I was on duty with my Kalashnikov when the men came into the yard. They were being chased and warned me that another group was after them, and that is why they jumped into our yard for cover.

Among the local populous it was rumoured that Mr. Simkins was working for the Central Intelligence Agency (CIA). This was the common belief among the citizenry toward all American foreigners. Suspicion of every foreigner was at an all time high. Anti-American sentiment was strong, and blame for anything was usually shared between Israel and the United States.

As mentioned earlier, Rachel had a young Lebanese woman working for her in the UN program. The young woman would translate and write letters in Arabic for Rachel. The woman had a boyfriend that no one liked and many referred to as a "pothead." He was a smuggler. Mr. Simkins would spend much of his time in the field; the boyfriend would come anytime he wished to take his girlfriend away, and threatened Rachel if she would tell anyone. He would say to Rachel, "If you tell anyone I will shoot you."

He was a trouble maker and liked to intimidate others. One time he came into the Simkins villa accompanied by his girlfriend.

Thinking they were there on business I allowed them to pass. Once inside the house, the boyfriend put his pistol to Mr. Simkins head who was in the kitchen. His girlfriend ran from the house. I came in from outside with my Kalashnikov, standing next to him I told him in Arabic that I was going to break his head. He then put away his pistol, but asked for a hammer. "What do you need a hammer for?" I asked. He took out a marble and said to me, "To break this marble." He broke the marble with the hammer to show Mr. Simkins the hashish inside it. He said to Mr. Simkins, "You think we are dumb, we are much smarter than you Americans. You cannot stop us."

At that instant my friend with a German four-wheel drive vehicle recognized the smugglers car and pulled over, he held his Kalashnikov in the air and fired several bursts. After that our intruder left. I came outside to thank my friend and let him know that everything was fine. Unknowing to any of us was that Mary Louis had her young daughter hide in the closet, had loaded both chambers of Mr. Simkins shotgun, and was standing in the hallway just outside the kitchen with the gun raised and ready. She said after the incident that she would have, "Given him both barrels." Her growing up on a Kansas farm where it was common to go hunting with a shotgun had paid off. The whole incident took place in only fifteen minutes.

When the boyfriend left the villa he was upset that his girlfriend had left him. I could see in the distance him shootiing at her with his pistol. I could see the bullets hitting the ground around her. He was trouble. Only days after this incidence, the smuggler boyfriend slowed down as he drove by. I stood there with my Kalashnikov raised and ready.

Smugglers were becoming inventive in ways to get their product to their buyers. Some smugglers sold to Egypt via Israel. One smuggler was stopped in Europe when it was discovered there was hashish in his gasoline tank. To reach greater markets smugglers had to find more inventive ways to import their drugs. Drug trafficking was a lucrative and booming world market.

As I have mentioned, Mr. Simkins' job was to interact, learn, and try to persuade growers of hashish to consider alternative crops, to grow food crops instead. Mr. Simkins was periodically invited to the home and hospitality of local growers and smugglers, this happened while his daughters were visiting.

During the visit the elder patriarch of the smuggler family where we were guests, decided that he would like my seventeen year old blond haired and blue eyed American sister to join his household. He even went so far as to say that he would consider kidnapping her. Since none of the Simkins family could speak or understand the native language, I warned them that we had to leave immediately. The patriarch was near his fifties in age.

Diplomatic license made of heavy aluminum used in Lebanon

As I speak of my father, mother, brothers and sisters, I am referring to my American adopted family. I have lost contact with my Afghan family. I now consider my American family my family. Until I received American citizenship it would have been risky for me to try and contact my biological siblings in Afghanistan. I was in fear of the two years mandatory service in the Afghan military required of every male Afghan. As mentioned earlier, that is why the government registers make an annual visit to the mountain villages to register new births, especially of males. If the child was a male Hazara two years were added to his birth year so he would go into the military sooner.

CHAPTER FOUR

THE INEVITABLE WAR

By the spring of 1975 serious conflicts had begun between Christians and Muslims. There were many Palestinian refugees in Lebanon estimated to be about ten percent of Lebanon's population. The presence of the Palestinian Liberation Organization (PLO) militants, were a direct factor in the agitation and growing conflicts. I began guarding the Simkins house at night and followed Mr. Simkins during the day, acting as his body guard.

Aware of the Christian and Muslim coexistence that predominated in the country, Mr. Simkins asked Abdulla, his counterpart on the project who was employed by the Lebanese government, if someday they might fight each other. Abdulla assured him that would not happen, and added, "We are like brothers." Most persons did not consider the thought of a full scale war ever happening between the groups.

It was the policy of the project to balance jobs and duties equally between Christians and Muslims. For instance, four drivers were needed to operate the four international Scout vehicles utilized in Baalbek. Four wheel drive vehicles were needed for the rough terrain. Two drivers hired were Christian, the other two were Muslim. One Muslim driver befriended one of the Christian drivers. Months later during late summer of 1975, when hostilities were rampant, the Muslim driver prewarned his Christian friend, to take his family and leave the area immediately because he knew there was going to be hostilities. The Christian driver's home was burned within a day of him being warned.

One day as I was guarding the Simkins villa, one of the young engineers working in our project for the Lebanese government, named Namatole, parked his car in front of the villa and came to the locked gate to talk. He asked a lot of questions, most centering around how Mr. Simkins managed the finances of his program, how it was funded, etc. I asked Namatole, "Do you have a meeting with Mr. Simkins?" His reply was, "No, I wanted to talk to you." We did some small talk, and then he asked me if I would consider working with him on a plan. And that plan was to kidnap Mr. Simkins and his family. Since I was working close to Mr. Simkins, acting as his body guard, he knew that I would be strategic to his plot, and hoped I would be willing to help. The engineer insisted that it would make us both rich.

Namatole was a challenge as an employee. He would be late and on occasion not show up. This would make Mr. Simkins upset and swear. Namatole did not like authority, and therefore did not like Mr. Simkins. Namatole is what you would call in the United States a trouble maker. No one liked him. He also made no effort to hide that he was a Communist. Rachel worked in the same office with Namatole, and he kept trying to get a date with her, but she never trusted his intentions. He would on occasion make threats against her, saying that he would beat her up, or even kill her.

At first when I heard Namatole's plan, I thought he was joking. But as we continued to talk over the gate I knew he was serious. He repeated his plan to me. I assured him that I would never be interested in such an action. Mr. Simkins was my employer I was here to protect him. Namatole then tried to belittle me, and said, "You're nothing." Our conversation got heated and we begin to swear in Arabic at each other. I told him that if he got close to Mr. Simkins or his family, I would *kassir rasak*, break his head. With the conflicts going on in Lebanon at the time, Namatole must have felt he could get away with such an act.

Namatole responded with anger saying, "I will kill you and them (referring to the Simkins)." I reciprocated, "Before you get me, I will get you first." My confidence was high; I was in good physical shape and taught Karate. He warned me that he had a pistol, which he always carried with him. He also had another in his car. I had been sitting at the entrance to the house when Namatole arrived. I had a Kalashnikov leaning against the wall that he could not see. To counter his threat, I responded that I would call six of my friends to come and help me.

Namatole responded back by saying, "You're blood is in my pocket!" He meant he had enough money at his disposal to hire someone to kill me. During this growing absence of law and order, it was not uncommon for someone to ask if there was someone who you did not like, that they would kill them for you, of course for a price. The price they would accept amounted to little more than one hundred dollars in American currency. The pending war had already eroded the respect for life.

I had one friend in particular that was my age from a wealthy smuggler family. As I mentioned earlier, he had a German made four wheel drive vehicle, on which the window folded down to allow you to shoot while driving. I threatened Namatole with his help. My friend was one of my students that I taught Karate. On occasion we would go places together. He always told me that if anyone ever wanted to hurt me to call him. After this incident with Namatole I went everywhere with Mr. Simkins and his family.

I could not believe that Namatole had proposed such a thing, and obviously did not understand the close relationship that I had established with Mr. Simkins and his family. I had accepted them as my own family. When I told Namatole that I would not even consider such a plan, he said he could get others to agree to help him. I made it clear to Namatole that if he came too close to any of my American family that he would have to go through me. He never approached me again on such a matter.

Not more than a week later, while riding the Simkins horse I saw Namatole in the distance coming toward me in his car. Ever since I had been shot at while riding the horse I carried Mr. Simkins double barrel shotgun with me. It was mounted on the side of the horse. When I saw Namatole coming down the street in his car, I jumped off the horse and grabbed the shotgun. He slowed as he saw me, but then kept going. Since I was close to the Simkins villa I decided to jog the rest of the way carrying the shotgun and pacing beside Harb.

Life went on, at least in the Bekaa Valley area where we lived. Most of the unrest and conflicts were occurring in or near Beruit. Residents in Beruit were taking precautions. They tried to stay home and did not go out at night. Checkpoints and road blocks were becoming a nuisance. There were separate checkpoints and roadblocks going into Christian areas, Muslim Areas, Druze areas, etc. If someone was not of that community, they would hastily turn around and flee, many times with check point guards firing at their vehicle. (See Appendix, A Personal Account of the Civil War in Lebanon)

There would be burning tires piled across the road to prevent anyone from going through a roadblock. If you tried to run it, the fire could explode your vehicle's fuel tank. During the war many incidents occurred at the roadblocks. What was disconcerting and caused many of these checkpoint shootings was that the state issued national identifications which listed your religion. You would have no hope if you found yourself at a Muslim checkpoint, and you were a Christian and your identification proved it. You learned where to go and where not to go. If you saw a roadblock ahead you would quickly consider your options. If you were unsure about it, you would be best to turn around before you got too close.

You could feel the thickening tension, the caution being taken, and the increase in violent incidents in the area. We were at the eve of the breakout of a full war but most were in disbelief, and it still seemed surreal to everyone. In Mr. Simkins own words, "Originally the fighting was primarily in and around Beirut, but as it escalated, the area around Bait Chama became ever more dangerous." He relates that at times they were shot at, "On one occasion, when we were returning from a trip to Beirut, we had to go through an area where there was fighting all around. Praying for our lives, we crouched down on the floor in the back of the car while my driver Ali, shouted I'm going to be killed, I'm going to be killed!" Through his skilful driving he got us out of the turmoil.

The full breakout of the civil war between Muslims and Christians began almost overnight. On April 13, 1975 an incident occurred that sparked serious repercussions. On that morning gunmen fired on a bus at an East Beirut Christian church, which killed four people. Just hours later, there was reciprocation when thirty Palestinians traveling in the same area were killed.

Clashes then erupted throughout the city of Beirut. Skirmishes continued and checkpoints were setup in each group's area. Because of retaliations, Christians fled to Christian areas and Muslims to Muslim areas. Then on December 6, 1975, which became known as Black Saturday, four Christian sect members were killed. This prompted the Christians to setup roadblocks throughout Beirut, and identification cards were checked for religious affiliation. Many Palestinians and Muslims were killed at road blocks. The war became a sectarian conflict.

Most people have not been in an armed conflict or an actual civil war that has taken place around them with real consequences. During such political or social unrest, citizens still need to live as best they can given their circumstances. They need to try to cling onto as many routines possible to support their life and family. There are days, or even weeks, that you may not be able to leave your home for fear of personal consequences.

Because of escalated conflicts and fighting, during the summer of 1975 things would shut down for days or weeks then be open the next depending on the intensity and location of the fighting. With the increased fighting banks were closed for weeks, which in essence shut down the country. The fighting in Beirut kept people huddled in their homes with supplies that ran thin. Mr. Simkins used a bank in Beirut where the main headquarters of the FOA was located. As the Project Manager of the UN mission he had overhead and staff to pay. One day the news media reported that banks and many other services would be open for the day.

It was a window of opportunity to cash the check that Mr. Simkins was holding. Since it would be much too obvious for Mr. Simkins himself, a white American to do this in the war torn country, I would do all the necessary errands. I knew my way around the area and Beirut, and fit in better as a local. Besides, as I have mentioned because of my Hazara features, and that I was a karate instructor many who did not know me thought that I was Japanese.

During this one day break in the fighting, which gave people a chance to resupply household necessities and services, Mr. Simkins gave me a check to cash at a bank in Beirut. Beirut was about fifty miles from the Bekaa Valley villa and usually took a little over an hour to drive. I left with Ahmed, one of Mr. Simkins' drivers in a Scout. At the bank I found large lines and had to wait three hours before we were able to get to a teller. I had not opened the envelope Mr. Simkins gave to me containing the check, I just handed it to the teller without really examining it. I got money from the teller and we headed back to Bekaa Valley.

I was excited to let Mr. Simkins know we had got the money, so when almost halfway back I called him on a pay phone. When I told him that we had a thousand pounds in cash, he told me that the check was written for ten thousand pounds. Mr. Simkins did not tell me to go back, but I was so upset I immediately turned around back to the bank. Ahmad was devastated by my decision and repeated his concerns for his life and his children.

We arrived at the bank but found it closed. I banged on the door until it was opened and I was finally let in, but I had to wait until the bank counted the day's receipts before they would do anything for me. Finally, they gave me the additional money we had not received. When I returned to the car the sun was setting, I found Ahmed weeping and repeatedly sobbing about his children, that they would not have a father. He was worried because we had to travel back in the dark. Ahmed had six children.

Ahmed through his driving experience knew different routes to take to avoid roadblocks and check points. There were Druze, Christian, and Muslim roadblocks between us and Bait Chama. As I mentioned many checkpoints would pile used tires across the road and set them on fire. We drove through one road block and were shot at. We had taken several Kalashnikovs with us in the Scout but did not return any fire. Ahmed was sobbing and wailing so much about his family, and repeating that we would be killed, that I took over driving.

Ahmed continued to whimper in the backseat repeating, "Who's going to feed my children? You're going to die with me!" We took as many alternative routes as we knew, and turned off our headlights. At one point we barreled through a chain link fence which protected a vineyard.

Finally we arrive back at the Bait Chama villa after five hours of death defying driving and maneuvering, and taking alternate routes. It would have been normally a scenic hour long trip. The Simkins were worried for our safety and were standing just inside the gate waiting for us when we arrived about ten o'clock.

Around this same time in early September, the Simkins son George and his fiancé were coming to visit his parents and youngest sister in Lebanon. George was in his early twenties at the time and visited for about ten days before returning to the United States to attend the University of Minnesota. He ultimately pursued a Doctorate in Agronomy like his father.

The night before George arrived there was a knock on the door of the Simkins house. Mr. Simkins thought it was me, but when he opened the door he found three men standing there with guns and masks. Mr. Simkins slammed the heavy self-locking door; he gave a quick motion to his wife to get out of the way. At that instant one of the gunmen fired two rounds through the thick wood door. The rounds went all the way through the house. Mrs. Simkins and her daughter had hastily took refuge in the hallway which had concrete walls.

It is unlikely that this was a random act because Mr. Simkins was known by many. They knew he was an American working in the area. Mr. Simkins gathered his wife and daughter and they huddled together in a back bedroom the rest of the night. All through the night Mr. Simkins worried that the gunmen would return. Gunfire and commotion continued throughout the night.

Mrs. Simkins discussed a plan with her eleven year old daughter. She told Sally that if anything happened that night, she should run out the back of the house and hide in the vineyard until I came, then go with me to the airport. Sally was to hide under one of the grape plants. The vines, which reached to the ground, would hide her. Mary Louise instructed her daughter to stay hid until, "Joe came." I was to pick up George and his fiancé at the airport the next day. Given the seriousness of the situation and their few options, it was a good plan. The landlord required Mr. Simkins to replace the door that had been shot through that fateful night.

At midnight I heard automatic weapons firing in the air, shouting, noise, and the stepping of thousands of feet on the street outside my apartment. Looking out the window there were literally thousands of people with guns coming down the street. There were so many of them they were shoulder to shoulder abreast, from one side of the street to the other. I did not know where they were all coming from. They may have come from the training camps in the mountains. I assumed they were mostly Palestinians marching in to terrorize the town because it was mostly Christian. Everyone carried guns. They evidently started in one village and as they moved through an area would attract more persons who would join and follow along, therefore the force kept growing.

It was noted later that all the Christians in the village that night had either fled to safer areas for refuge, or remained as insignificant as possible in their homes. Christian teachers, store owners, employees were all gone. The Christian phone operator, who came to teach Sally Arabic, had left her station for safety. After the event we inquired about the Christian operator but never heard from her again.

My first thought was of the Simkins. They were Americans and these armed persons were Muslims, inundated with Palestinians. I tried desperately to get to the Simkins house but there were virtually too many armed persons marching down the street, and I was constantly detained and questioned if I were a Muslim. Checkpoints had been established that were little more than a hundred yards apart. There were so many armed persons going by on the street that it took me about four hours, from checkpoint to checkpoint, to go one mile from my apartment to the Simkins villa.

It was obvious that I dare not inquire about the Simkins or the events taking place, otherwise I would have been labeled a sympathizer, and the consequences could have been disastrous. I did not arrive at the Simkins home until just before day break.

As I arrived I knew something had taken place when I saw the gate wide open, and the cars outside with their doors also open. A jolt went through me thinking the Simkins had been harmed, or worse yet kidnapped. Luckily, as I came into the yard the family saw me and let me in the house. I could not help but notice the bullet holes in the door.

It was reported later that about ten thousand Muslims, mostly Palestinians had marched through the Bekaa Valley area that night. The next day when George was to arrive all was quiet. The thousands of persons with guns were gone and the Lebanese military had taken control. They had set up a checkpoint in the middle of the village. I remember there was a light hanging down at the checkpoint so guards could see faces and identifications at night. I recall that the bulb had been shot out. The Lebanese military remained in the area several weeks.

I would stay at the Simkins house quite often, but prior to this incident it had been relatively quiet so I chose to stay at my apartment that evening. One thing that helped me that night weaving among the mass of soldiers and checkpoints, is that many times I was thought to be *Yabani*, Japanese or *Cini*, Chinese. At the time karate movies were popular and there had been a recent hijacking by a Japanese Marxist group in nearby Israel.

The next morning Mr. Simkins did not show up at his office in Baalbek. Everyone in the office was concerned about him since it was uncommon for him to miss a day, especially without notice. He later shared with his staff that he had to stay home to replace a door on his home, and explained to them what had happened. It had been a long and eventful night for the Simkins, and had Mr. Simkins not slammed the door closed to the masked gunmen, he and his family would have suffered grave consequences.

About the same time, the well, used to irrigate the crops on the American University of Beruit (AUB) experimental farm, was blown up. The experimental farm was a cooperative between the American University and Lebanon. They would experiment with methods of fertilization, crop rotation, irrigation, and raising dairy cattle. The farm was only a mile away from the Simkins Bekaa Valley villa. Agricultural tractors and equipment were also stolen.

From the Baalbek office, the four International Scout vehicles used for the project were stolen, only to be seen days later with their cabs cut off and gun emplacements installed. It was almost comical to see the Scouts at a roadblock with their cabs off and guns installed, while still displaying United Nations decals on their sides.

After the incident of the gunmen shooting through his door, Mr. Simkins arranged to have a guard twenty four hours a day at his residence. For most of the day I was the guard then a friend of Ali, named Abraham, the other guard. Abraham replaced me each evening from seven o'clock to midnight. This gave me a break and time to rest.

There was no question that things were heating up in Bekaa Valley, hostilities were on the rise. Palestinian training camps were located in the mountains surrounding the valley. The Israelis would periodically bomb the camps. The valley was a large area for the dwindling Lebanese military and local police forces to oversee.

In early September 1975 George and his fiancé arrived and I

brought them to Bait Chama from the airport just after the incident of the men shooting through the Simkins door. George and his fiancé stayed two days at the villa. The next several days the family traveled to neighboring countries. They visited Syria and Jordan for two days each and made their base in Damascus. The family thought it best they stay away from their Bekaa Valley home for a while.

Although random incidents continued, and there were few days that went by without hearing gunfire in the distance, people adjusted to the environment. Guns were becoming more common in Lebanon, and gunfire was heard often. It was not uncommon to hear a gun discharge somewhere. It is difficult to explain, we just learned to accept it. There was a certain level of acceptance, because life had to go on. But at the same time random attacks were on the rise.

Many people began to carry Kalashnikov's. It was not unusual to hear rapid gunfire in celebration of something. If someone had a birthday, and they happen to live on third floor, a window would simply be opened and the Kalashnikov thrust out and several bursts of rounds fired into the air. This behavior was accepted and no one challenged the action.

Guarding the Simkins villa with the Simkins double barrel shotgun

69

As I mentioned, despite the unrest, it seemed business as usual. What none of us realized was that we were only days away from a full scale civil war between Christians and Muslims. There were still tourists coming to Lebanon and Beirut, and George thought at the time that being an American tourist helped. However, being an American in those areas no longer shields you. Americans in Arab countries must remain cautious and unobtrusive and follow cultural norms.

One time while driving in Beirut with George, his fiancé, Ali and myself we stopped for a red light, only yards from the guard gate of a foreign embassy of another Arab country. There was an armed guard on duty. An Arab man was having a verbal confrontation with the guard. The man was obviously agitated about something. The next instant, the guard in one swift movement lowered his gun and shot the man! We were shocked by the incident. Georges' first reaction was as a tourist, to take a picture but I stopped him. It could have cost us our lives. I shouted at Ali who was driving, "GO! GO!" He was momentarily froze by the incident, but then sped away through the red light. This all occurred in a moment.

Another time when George and his fiancé were exploring the area on foot, his fiancé was hit by a passerby. It is not unusual for women to be hit in Arab countries, especially those not conforming to social norms. An American woman especially at the time, wearing a short sleeve low cut blouse, and no head dress would have stood out. In other words, if you are a woman in an Arab country do not show too much skin, and try to blend in as much as possible.

During George's stay we were invited to another major smuggler's house to visit. The smugglers are the go-betweens from producers to dealers, and sell worldwide. The smugglers we visited were Christian. Mr. Simkins found it easier to work with the Christian hashish growers and smugglers. We interacted and they introduced George to the traditional water pipe. Tragically, the smuggler's family we visited was all killed in the civil war.

70

Myself, Mr. Simkins behind me, and George smoking a traditional water pipe

We drove directly from Damascus to a hotel in Beirut a day before George had to be at the airport. We would spend almost two weeks at the hotel. During this time Mr. Greensheafs, who was the UN project head out of Washington D.C., flew in on a routine visit with Mr. Simkins, and stayed for several days with us at the hotel. Mr. Simkins updated him on the project in Lebanon and the escalated fighting. Originally from Oklahoma, Mr. Greensheafs later became a consultant to the World Bank and stayed involved in an international drug eradication program.

The following day I brought George and his fiancée to the airport with Mr. Simkins riding along. The day after, I drove Mr. Greensheafs to the airport, this time Mr. Simkins was advised not to go along since fighting had elevated. There were also fewer and fewer flights because foreign airlines did not want to put their planes at risk. We were only about eighty miles from Damascus to the east, but there was no way we would make it going overland through checkpoints and active fighting. We would have to fly to get out of the country.

Luckily the military was holding the airport, but we did not know for how long. The airport would close then reopen without any regularity; it all depended on the degree of fighting. Army units were breaking up. By late September desertions were widespread reducing the effectiveness of the military. Soldiers would simply go their own way, Christians to their areas, and Muslims to theirs, bringing with them what equipment resources they could from the army they had deserted. This caused the country to be lawless.

While we were staying at the hotel, the Simkins daughter learned how to play bridge. Always the caring teacher, Mary Louise taught Sally the card game. This was Mrs. Simkins way to keep her daughter occupied and help focus her away from the reality of what was happening around them. We had two adjacent rooms. Mr. Simkins and I were in one, with Mrs. Simkins and her daughter in the other. Each time we heard automatic weapons, and bullets going through the hotel walls, or a nearby explosion, Mr. Simkins would check the safety of his family in the next room. His wife and daughter stayed huddled in the middle of the room away from windows to avoid stray bullets. Snipers were everywhere and a constant threat.

Each day there were fewer people in the hotel. Eventually we were the only ones left, and little service remained. Food supplies had dwindled to where there were only carrots and beans to eat. Knowing the uncertainty of our situation, I kept devising and reanalyzing strategies in my head. We could not go back to Bait Chama. We had to fly out. The fighting and bombing continued all around. No one could be trusted. I was trying to conceive every scenario for our survival, even to consider covering our heads and dressing like the locals. I dwelled for days on what to do. A small crew of workers remained in the hotel only because they were afraid to go home through the fighting.

In my nineteen years I had learned how to fend for myself, beginning at an early age, and by the time I had left Afghanistan to travel to Iran I was seasoned in the art of self sufficiency. But now I had the fate of this American family on my shoulders. We were in an escalating civil war and things were deteriorating by the hour. I had to formulate a plan how to get to the airport. I felt the responsibility to keep the Simkins safe and to get them out of this predicament.

Finally I devised a workable plan to get everyone to the airport. I knew we had to leave the next morning; the fighting was ongoing and would only get worse.

Mr. Simkins kept calling the American embassy, which was less than a mile from our hotel but the embassy was in no position to help us. Given the active fighting they said they could not send anyone to help us. Following his conversation with the embassy Mr. Simkins said, "I will give a million dollars to take my family out of here!" After we were denied help from the embassy, we knew we were truly on our own.

The night before we were to leave, the hotel was bombed. Our rooms were on the third level, we felt the whole building shake from the explosion which destroyed its upper level. The smell of smoke permeated all through the hotel. We were close to the largest hotel, the Saint George on the Christian side of an invisible line. A line that changed with the fighting and was later referred to as the "green line." The term came about in reference to the green vegetation that covered the small demarcation that separated the two main fighting factions.

Opposite the Saint George was a Holiday Inn held by Muslim forces. Rockets and small arms fire were exchanged between the two hotels. We could see gun emplacements on the adjacent hotel and other buildings. Because of this exchange we received stray rounds and rockets. The fighting between the hotels would later be referred to as, "The battle of the Hotels" in the Lebanese civil war.

The hotel where we were staying was on the coast. It was ironic that one day there were hundreds of boats in the harbor, but by the next day there were none. They had all left overnight. The Simkins Chevrolet was parked in back of the hotel, the side

73

which faced the ocean. I would periodically check on the vehicle. To protect the gasoline in our vehicle from being siphoned, I put on a locking gas cap I purchased the last time I filled the Chevrolet. With the war raging on, gasoline was not available and became a precious commodity. We needed to be sure we had enough fuel to get to the airport. Under the circumstances we could not trust anyone.

I asked two Christian taxi drivers I had befriended while working at the antique store, if they would drive us to the airport. They turned me down because they knew there was a Palestinian refugee settlement between Beirut and the airport. It had been sponsored by the Lebanese government. They knew as Christians they would have little chance if captured.

I then called another friend named Ahmed who I also met through the antique store. He was one of the taxi drivers who would bring tourists to the store. We had become good friends and Ahmed was Muslim. Although reluctant at first to bring us to the airport; my urging along with my promise to drive another car as a lead vehicle, and a sum of money from Mr. Simkins, enticed him enough to help us.

The next morning, my taxi cab friend and I started our mini convoy first to the United Nations office near the airport to drop off the Simkins Chevrolet. Mrs. Simkins and her daughter wore a head covering to hide their hair, the daughter was blond. We went swiftly to the vehicles trying to draw the least attention. Kidnappings and sniping were rampant.

I drove ahead in the Simkins Chevrolet to take the attention and make sure the trail was safe and open to pass. We kept a distance between our vehicles so if I would encounter a road block or ambush the taxi had time to turn around. At times I traveled eighty miles an hour through the streets of Beirut dodging any obstacles in the road. We went through the "embassy row" of Beirut. There was persistent automatic weapons fire, explosions, and rockets that seemed to be happening all around us. I had little time to think, only react and rely on my senses and adrenalin which permeated through my body.

At one instance, encountering a long curve on the route, I was going so fast my tires screeched and the car skidded toward the curb. The curb was the only thing keeping me from the sea below.

The Simkins daughter, eleven years old at the time remembers lying on the floor of the taxi as it sped through the streets of Beirut; both parents covered Sally with their bodies to protect her. It was the ride of her life. I kept ahead until we got to the UN building. We were able to drop off the Chevrolet and all go in the taxi to the airport. Ahmed left after delivering us safely to the airport. He was a father of several children, to this day I still wonder what happened to him. Did he make it back safely through all the turmoil, bombs, automatic weapons fire and road blocks? He once told me he had friends in the Palestinian camp near Beirut. I hope he was able to make it to the camp safely, I never heard from him again.

After our heralding ride through an active war zone we got to the airport only to find it in chaos. The airport was filled with men, women, and children. We heard all languages spoken among the crowd. Many Lebanese were also trying to leave their country. People were shouting, crying, shoving, screaming and swearing, pushing and fighting. It was disconcerting to see the behaviors displayed by fellow human beings under the stress, uncertainty, fear for their lives, and desperation of the situation.

Guards struggled to keep order. As I mentioned, since the start of the war the airport would be closed and then opened again depending on the fighting. This could happen almost at a moment's notice. We saw there were few airplanes parked at the airport. This was unusual in comparison to the Beirut airports normal busy operation. Usually there were planes taxiing, taking off, and landing every so many minutes.

The hours we had to wait seemed like days and were coupled with uncertainty. All we could do was sit and wait not knowing our fate from minute to minute. Would they close the airport? Would we be able to get on the next plane? We were scarred and not sure how we would come out of this, we kept praying. Mr. Simkins evidently through a combination of cash and diplomatic clout was finally able to get tickets for all of us on the next flight. Fewer and fewer airlines were giving service to Beirut. There were so many people and so few flights.

We waited eight long hours before a flight arrived. It was wrought with hours of uncertainty, chaos, fear, and demoralized spirits. And all the while in the not so distant background we heard the endless blasts of bombs from the active fighting in Beirut. We were exhausted, we had not slept for days, nor had we eaten much. We waited all day just for a thirty minute flight to Damascus. Mrs. Simkins and her daughter Sally, spent the time writing long letters to friends and relatives, this helped take the focus off of our reality. There was the constant plaguing question, deep in our thoughts, if we were going to make it.

The Air France plane landed, loaded, and took off right away, so as to spend as little time as possible on the ground. The war was raging at the fringes of the airport. Inside the plane fear was evident on everyone's face. Adults and children were crying and whimpering in fear. It was overbooked and noisy in the plane, people were everywhere, sitting on laps and in the aisle because there were no seats left. No one was able to take any luggage.

We did not feel safe yet, because at any moment our plane could have been hit by a rocket. As the plane gained altitude and circled around Beirut, setting its course for Damascus we looked out windows in disbelief, the city was all ablaze.

We learned later that our flight was the last flight out of Beirut before the airport closed for days. It was difficult not to think about the many persons still at the airport when we left, who were unable to get on our flight. Only thirty minutes, the time it took to fly to Damascus, separated us from consequences I do not wish to think about.

Our flight landed in Damascus, Syria. The moment the tires touched the tarmac there was instantaneous shouts of relief and jubilation. The realization that we had just come from a raging civil war, with bursts of automatic weapons fire, explosions and translucent trails of rockets, to the sanctity and relative quiet of the airport in Damascus was just setting in. Most of the people on the flight had to leave with what they had, or were able to carry on board. Looks on faces went from uncertainty and fear, to hope.

Just as the plane came to a stop, Mrs. Simkins threw her arms around me, kissed me and said, "You'll be my son Joe!"

I had saved them, and my efforts would continue to keep them out of harm's way. I knew the culture; I understood its ways and spoke the language. The Simkins were white, obviously American, and stood out compared to the general population. The embrace and kiss that Mrs. Simkins gave me, that moment on the plane immediately after we had landed, was a compassionate thank you, and a deeper acceptance of me as would a natural parent. It was a turning point, and I was adopted into their family. Once off the plane we all had Baklava. After a week of dwindling food supplies at the hotel, and the loss of appetite from stress and worry, the sweet taste of the dessert was reinforcement to us that we were finally safe.

With the exodus of people leaving Lebanon and how packed our flight had been, we knew the hotels would fill quickly. However, we were fortunate enough to find a hotel where we stayed for three nights in Damascus.

After experiencing the fighting in Beirut which had spread to Bekaa Valley and across Lebanon, the Simkins thought it best to stay away from their Bait Chama residence for a while in hopes that things would settle down. It was late September and Abdulla accompanied the Simkins on a road trip to Turkey. Mr. Simkins left Abraham and I in charge of their house and property. I was given the Volvo to drive which had diplomatic immunity.

While the Simkins were gone the two civil engineers working for him from Cyprus, who had an apartment in Baalbek, were severely beaten. One was beat so bad and face so swollen that his eye was almost closed. They were concerned for their life. They pleaded with me to take them out of the area for fear they would not live to see another day. I drove both engineers to Damascus for their safety. They eventually returned home to Cyprus.

On an earlier occasion I came to pick up one of the engineers and was shot at in the diplomatic Volvo. My immediate defense reaction was to put the gearshift in reverse and bolt backward, this was an automatic reflex and I hit a pole. I left the scene and returned to the Simkins villa. Because of the extensive damage to the vehicle I told Mr. Simkins that I had been chased. Mr. Simkins was upset with me for the damage to the Volvo. Repairs were not easily done and parts not readily available, especially in the war torn environment. Later Rachel had to move from her apartment in Baalbek to Damascus. Baalbek was predominantly Muslim.

I left Damascus to return to the Bait Chama villa to resume my guard duty. At the same time, the Simkins and Abdulla were coming back from their trip. They were unaware of the violence that had taken place. Returning to the villa I passed the Scout coming from the opposite direction. We passed each other in Bait Chama. I honked my horn and blinked my lights to get their attention. I turned around to warn them about the fighting and events that had occurred while they were gone. There had been increased violence since they left.

As I caught up to them I shouted, "What the hell you doing here! Do you know what is going on?" They were unaware of the events taking place in Bekaa Valley. We talked briefly and they followed me to the villa. There they freshened up and grabbed items from the house. Abdulla drove the Scout to his home. The rest of us got in the Volvo to go to Damascus. Given the events of the past several days, we felt we would be safest in Damascus. We traveled less than ten miles toward the Syrian border when we saw a roadblock in the distance. We saw the black smoke ahead of burning tires and turned around immediately. Within the hour that had occurred from when I had passed the Simkins in their Scout, followed them to the villa, and then joined me in the Volvo, there had been a roadblock setup. I had traveled the same road just an hour before, and there had been no roadblock.

We were forced to go back to Bait Chama. I was concerned the Simkins would be kidnapped if we stopped at the roadblock. We stayed at the villa for the night, and hoped things would settle down. But that night, there was a lot of shooting all around us. We left the next morning for Damascus. The day was quiet and no shots were heard. I drove the Volvo, and the Simkins and their daughter all laid low in the backseat to limit their profile.

Thinking things would settle down we stayed in Damascus. Mr. Simkins and I would spend the days in his office in Baalbek, and return to Damascus toward evening. We checked on the villa almost every day. On one of our trips Mr. Simkins brought grapes from the villa vineyard to the border guards we passed daily. One time when returning to Damascus, we were detained by the border guards on the Syrian side for several hours. When we finally reached Damascus we found out what had caused the delay. Three Palestinian men were hung in a town square. The bodies remained there for several days.

A few days later the Simkins returned to the villa for several days, but finding it not safe they decided to go to Turkey.

When we left Beirut on the last flight out, we had to leave everything at the house in Bait Chama. As they say, "We left with only the clothes on our backs." My American mother wept at the thought of having to leave family pictures and early movies of her children, family heirlooms, clothes, and household items. We had to also leave behind the six Persian rugs that my American mother cherished and wished to hand down to her children. The Simkins purchased the rugs while in Iran, during Mr. Simkins first assignment abroad.

The Simkins had approached living in Lebanon as they had all their other assignments. They brought with them their pictures, movies, and mementos of their children growing up. They never anticipated the events that would take place and the civil war in which they found themselves. They did not consider the possibility that they would not complete their full five year term of their assignment in Lebanon.

I felt bad about the personal loses my American family had experienced. After our ordeal, few days went by without my American mother breaking down into tears thinking about all the family items they had left. Mary Louise kept thinking of the family heirlooms and irreplaceable gifts from her parents. I felt so bad for Mrs. Simkins that I decided to retrieve as many of the items as I could from their house in Bait Chama. I felt a personal responsibility to do this even thought the civil war was raging on in Lebanon.

When we returned to Damascus we found hotels filled, but managed to find a convent where we could stay. Staying in the convent was an experience for us; it was not what we were used to. We had left a spacious villa with a vineyard in its back and having all the facilities of a modern home. Food did not taste good at the convent, nor was it tidy, service was poor and it was over crowded.

The Convent was dedicated to Saint Paul. There was a statue of him on his horse. As written in doctrine, Paul was a Roman soldier of Jewish descent. As a Roman he would persecute the new Christians. One day on the road to Damascus to arrest Christians a blinding light flashed from the sky and knocked him off his horse, and he heard a voice speak to him. After this incident he became a missionary and spread the news of the new religion.

Each morning at the convent Christian Mass was held. I was used to this service since I would accompany the Simkins on Sunday mornings to a church in Lebanon. Given their situation the sisters tried to accommodate as many people as they could.

As I mentioned, hotels were filled to capacity because of all the displaced people from Lebanon who escaped the escalated civil war. We praised the sisters for their willingness to accommodate as many people as possible. Some nights I saw people sleeping in the hallway. Just about every day we would check on vacancies at the hotels but they remained full. We had to stay at the convent almost two months.

Mr. Simkins still needed to oversee the project that he headed, so after several days I started driving to the FAO office in Baalbek almost every day. Employees needed to be paid and the mail checked. One time also, I had Ali pick me up and bring me to the UN office in Beirut to get the Simkins Chevrolet we had left there. Each day I had to go through several roadblocks to go to the Baalbek office, and only stay for the day, making sure to return before dark. Hostilities continued in the area. Mr. Simkins was able to setup an office for his project in the United Nations in Damascus. With Rachel in Damascus much of the project was managed from there.

Rachel stayed in Damascus during the winter of 1975 where she found a roommate to share an apartment. She would have Ali pick her up in the diplomatic Volvo and drive her to Beirut to pick up mail from the UN office. They had to go through many checkpoints along the way, where men always pointed guns at them. At one checkpoint in Beirut that Ali was going to run, but Rachel pleaded with him to stop fearing they would be shot, the guards questioned Ali and inquired about his passenger. Ali told the guards that she was going to become part of his family. The guards allowed them to pass.

Rachel took these opportunities to visit her sister who lived in Beirut. Because of the shortages caused by the war, Rachel would bring fresh meat and vegetables from Damascus to her sister on these trips to the United Nations office in Beirut. Her sister and family were living on pasta and rice. When the staff at the UN office learned of this, they started placing orders with Rachel to bring on her next visit.

The Simkins invited me to come to the United States. They knew it would be difficult for me after they left. But my citizenship was a concern. I was still a citizen of Afghanistan but on visa to Lebanon. Mr. Simkins contacted the head at the American Embassy in Damascus. The embassy head was familiar with Mr. Simkins work and was curious about the UN project in Lebanon. He was interested in its progress. The embassy head asked Mr. Simkins, "What would it take to get a copy of your report?" Mr. Simkins obtained a visa for me simply by sharing his report on how the, "Crops for Drugs Program" was going in Lebanon. Both parties had benefited. The UN paid for my belongings to be shipped to America. Once in America I stayed with the Simkins at their home in a state called Minnesota.

In November 1975 Mr. Simkins flew to Pakistan where he was reassigned before coming to the United States. I flew with Mrs. Simkins and her daughter from Damascus to the United States. As we transferred in Frankfort, Germany a customs agent took my passport. He must have been suspicious since I was flying with two Americans and he did not understand the connection with us traveling together. The agent reiterated to Mrs. Simkins that I was from Afghanistan. Mary Louis held her own and told the customs agent that she was not going until, "Joe goes." A supervisor came and told the agent to return my passport and let me pass. Sally was in tears.

The following spring in April 1976, I flew with Mr. Simkins to Rome, Italy where the European headquarters of the FAO was located very near the Coliseum ruins. I continued on to Damascus, Syria by myself. Mr. Simkins went on to Pakistan where he had been reassigned. As had become the practice, Mrs. Simkins and their youngest daughter stayed back in the United States until Sally finished the school year, and then came to Damascus.

Rachel remained in Damascus supporting the FOA Lebanese program. Mr. Simkins spent five months in an opium growing area of Pakistan while the war waged in Lebanon. He was unable to return to Lebanon so Rachel and I managed the Bekaa Valley project from Damascus. I eventually rented an apartment in the new location.

For once in my life I had the life of ease. I was paid eight hundred Syrian pounds for my duty. I would visit Rachel in the morning to see if there was any mail to pick up at the office in Damascus, or any errands to run. I always asked Rachel if she had heard from Mr. Simkins. I had two diplomatic vehicles at my disposal and gasoline was supplied by the UN. The diplomatic vehicles gave me options that I would normally not have had. With them I could park virtually anywhere.

After checking in with Rachel, the rest of the day I would drive around and visit friends. Girls would also try to meet me. Police officers would salute me as I drove past because I was in a diplomatic vehicle. I began to make contacts with various businesses thinking that since I was going to return to the United States, I was considering an import business.

As time went on I was determined to get back as many of the items the Simkins had to leave in their Bekaa Valley home as I could. Mrs. Simkins was troubled by the loss of family memorabilia that could never be replaced. Damascus was only about forty miles from the Bait Chama villa. The Simkins had warned Rachel not to let me go to the former residence.

By June 1976, disregarding the warning directed to me by Rachel and the Simkins, I arranged with Ali to meet me with his car at the Syrian-Lebanon border. I took a taxi from Damascus to meet him. From the border Ali drove me to the Bait Chama villa. While driving we heard shooting and in the distance saw a military jeep flip over from an explosion. About the same time a bullet pinged through Ali's trunk. We fired back. I emptied a full clip of the Kalashnikov out my window as we swerved into the ditch.

Not sure where the automatic weapons fire was coming from, we stayed off the road until dark. We had taken three Kalashnikovs with us. We emptied several clips into the distance to let whoever know that we were armed. Ali then drove me to Abdulla's house where I stayed the night.

83

The next day Ali and I drove to the Simkins villa which we found in disarray. Boxes of slides of Mr. Simkins projects were strewn over the floor. It took Ali and I the whole day to pick up the slides and family memorabilia. The persons who had broken into the villa had held a gun on Abraham, the Simkins guard who was given the task of overseeing the residence while we were gone. We suspected that the persons who broke into the house were not looking for valuables but for anything to prove their suspicions that Mr. Simkins was a spy.

When we arrived at the villa, the elderly landlord came with a Kalashnikov and held it on me. His hands shook from age and I was afraid the gun would go off accidently because of his uncontrollable shaking. The elderly man continued to hold his gun on me and insisted that I fix up the house before I leave. The house had damage to the doors where the intruders had broken through. They had cut holes through the locked sliding doors of the bedrooms. The holes were cut large enough for a person to walk through.

Ali and I packed the many slides, family pictures and mementos, and tidied up the house. Most of the Lebanese slides had been taken. I was able to hire a carpenter to repair the damage for eight hundred Lebanese pounds. I had to borrow money from Ali, and had to sell some items from the house to raise enough money to pay the carpenter. When the job was finished the landlord gave me the six Persian rugs that he had brought to his house.

I stayed the night with a Lebanese judge that was an acquaintance of Mr. Simkins. His house was close to the border. I gave the judge a letter stating that he could have the washer and dryer from the Bait Chama house. The next day Ali and I traveled back in his vehicle to the Syrian border but the border guards would not let us pass. They wanted a customs fee for the rugs in Ali's car. My only option was to take a taxi back to Damascus and return with the diplomatic Volvo. I returned and loaded the Persian rugs, family photos, tapes, and mementos into the Volvo and drove back to Damascus with everything.

I visited Rachel and surprised her with the items from the Simkins house. Rachel, who had prewarned me that the Simkins did not want me to go to the Bait Chama villa, told me that Mrs. Simkins would be very upset with me. She arranged to ship everything back to the United States, where the Simkins were at the time. At the writing of this book, the Simkins children each have a rug. What interesting stories those rugs could tell if only they could talk.

The Lebanese civil war continued, and lasted over a decade.

In June 1976 the US Ambassador Francis E. Meloy, his economic counselor Robert O. Waring, and their Lebanese driver Mohammed Moghrabi, were kidnapped at a checkpoint while they crossed between the Christian and Muslim sectors in Beirut. Their bodies were found only hours later riddled with bullet holes in the Muslim Sector controlled by the Popular Front for the Liberation of Palestine. (See References in the Appendix)

Sadly, as Henry Kissinger describes in the declassified memorandum about the Ambassador's death, "He [the Ambassador] was on his way to meet with the new President Sarkis, to discuss the situation and possible U.S. evacuation."

The then US President Gerald R. Ford on June 17, 1976 made the following statement to reporters in the Briefing Room of the White House:

"The Assassination of our Ambassador in Beirut, Francis E. Meloy, Jr., and of our Counselor for Economic Affairs, Robert O. Waring, and of their driver is an act of senseless, outrageous brutality. I extend to their families my own deep sense of sorrow and that of all the American people.

These men were on their way to meet with President-elect Sarkis. They were on a mission of peace, seeking to do what they could in the service of their country to help restore order, stability, and reason to Lebanon. Their deaths add another tragedy to the suffering which the Lebanese people have endured beyond measure.

These men had lived with danger for many weeks and did so with dedication and disregard of personal safety, as we have come to expect of the Foreign Service.

The goals of our policy must remain unchanged. The United States will not be deterred in its search for peace by these murders. I have instructed Secretary Kissinger to continue our intensive efforts in this direction.

I will name a new Ambassador to Lebanon within the very near future to resume the mission of Ambassador Meloy, which he performed so brilliantly.

I have also instructed the Secretary to get in touch with all of the governments in the area and with the Lebanese leaders to help identify the murderers and to see that they are brought to justice.

I have also ordered that all appropriate resources of the United States undertake immediately to identify the persons or groups responsible for this vicious act.

Those responsible for these brutal assassinations must be brought to justice. At the same time, we must continue our policy of seeking a peaceful solution in Lebanon. That is the way we can best honor the brave men who gave their lives for this country and for the cause of peace." [1]

Following the murder of the American ambassador, on June 20, 1976 President Ford ordered the evacuation of one hundred sixteen Americans from Lebanon. Only essential people were left in the American Embassy in Beirut to maintain basic operations. (See the Declassified White House Memorandum in the Appendix)

The British Broadcasting Service (BBC) followed on the same day with their broadcast: "Westerners evacuated from Beirut." "Nearly 300 Westerners, mostly Americans and Britons, have been moved from Beirut and taken to safety in Syria by the US military."

After the announcement issued in 1976 by the United States government that American citizens were to be evacuated, and unable to visit Lebanon for their own safety, Rachel's sister, her sisters' Lebanese husband, and children came to the United States. Her sister worked in a hospital in Beirut. Rachel's sister was able to get a visa for herself and her children, but the person at the American embassy was hesitant at first to give her husband a visa.

They took the last flight out in late December 1975 just before the airport shutdown completely for almost two weeks. The Simkins were no longer able to return to their project in Lebanon and returned to the United States.

The Chevrolet owned by Mrs. Simkins had to be sold. Mr. Simkins told me that whatever I could get for it over four thousand dollars would be mine. Because Syrian citizens could not buy a car unless it was approved by the government, I went to Jordan to sell it. I was able to sell it for four thousand four hundred US dollars. The difference I was able to keep.

The Lebanon Civil War lasted from 1975 to 1990 and tens of thousands of Christian and Muslim lives were lost. It is estimated that about seven percent of the Lebanese population was killed during the civil war. It is also estimated that close to a million fled Lebanon during the initial years of the war 1975 to 1976.[2] By the end of 1975 it was uncertain which faction was dominant. The fighting occurred among many religious factions, which throughout the war were in and out of alliances with each other.

The roots of the war go back to the establishment of the State of Israel which displaced one hundred thousand Palestinian refugees to Lebanon, nearly ten percent of Lebanon's population. This gave them a political presence in the country. By the 1970s the armed Palestinian Liberation Organization (PLO) presence became obvious. The PLO had been entrenched in southern Lebanon since 1969. With arrival of PLO guerrilla forces inciting the Palestinian refugee population it sparked an uprising.

This led up to the April 13, 1975 incident previously mentioned, which is credited for the spark that ignited the war. With the apparent tension and armed groups it was a powder keg to explode.

Growing and smuggling drugs increased exponentially during the Lebanon civil war. There was less law and order. It is said that Lebanon became one of the world's largest drug producers at this time, with a good portion of hashish production coming from Bekaa Valley. Arms smuggling became a close second.

It is unfortunate that all the efforts, budget, and good will given to the United Nations program, designed to eradicate the production and distribution of hashish and opium at its source, was all for naught.

[1]*www.arlingtoncemetery.com*
[2]*www.globalsecurity.org*

CHAPTER FIVE

A MAN WITHOUT A COUNTRY

It was a dream come true when I was able to visit the United States on a tourist visa.

To remain in America, I had to keep renewing my visa, and would have to send my passport to the Afghan Embassy in Washington D.C. It was 1979, and my passport was due for another renewal, I sent it to the Afghan embassy, but this time they cancelled my passport. I was devastated. After risking my life, and finally making it to America and seeing all the freedoms and opportunities America had it seemed unreal. With my passport cancelled, my American father described me as, "A man without a country."

He was right. I truly felt in limbo, like a man without a country. But in my case I did have a country, but I did not want to go back to it.

There have been references to persons without a country in spy novels and war stories, and during the cold war when athletes would seek asylum. But until you have truly become a person without a country the reality really does not sink in. If you are in this situation your life is put on hold, your days calculated, and you have no immediate future plans or goals because there is so much uncertainty in your life.

This is how I felt. I have always been a positive person. I have always been able to see, like they say in America the potential, "pot of gold" at the end of a rainbow. But if you have no rainbow, is there still be a pot of gold to obtain?

The country I loved from the moment I stepped foot on its soil, the United States of America, I now had to leave because my passport was revoked. The country that I did not want to return to, that only discriminated against me and my culture, was still inflicting its misery on me.

My country of origin, Afghanistan was the last place that I wished to go. If I had to go back my life would return to subservience and my hopes shattered. Things had gone well for me the last several years. My unattainable goal of freedom, in the form of visiting the United States had become a reality. I had a taste of the individual empowerment that this country gives, and now it would be difficult to live without it.

But as my name implies, God's Gift, I had a very supportive adoptive family, with an American father that worked in international service through the United Nations. Mr. Simkins reassured to me several times saying, "One thing I am sure of, is that you will do well. I'm not worried about you, you'll survive." He knew I had ambition and drive, and those had usually been my hope. But this was different, it was beyond my level of control.

I was very concerned about my immigration status, with the thought hovering in my mind that I may have to return to my native land. I was worried, but would not consider returning to Afghanistan as an option. I had been able to stay away from Afghanistan since I had left almost a decade before. Despite worry about my dilemma, my American father tried to brighten the day by suggesting one way out for me would be to, "Marry a fat rich girl." It is one time my American father's humor did not give me uplift.

But, as luck has followed me, my American father was working in Washington D.C. at the time, and was able to personally carry my passport to the Afghan embassy in Washington. They renewed the passport for another year, that very same day. Mr. Simkins stressed to them that I needed to finish school.

In 1979 the Russians invaded my native Afghanistan, because of this incidence, as a twist of fate I could remain in the United States under refugee status. We contacted Rudy Boschwitz, the Minnesota Senator at the time to help us. My father knew him personally. We also hired a lawyer.

From there on I was able to renew my passport annually, until I received my US citizenship.

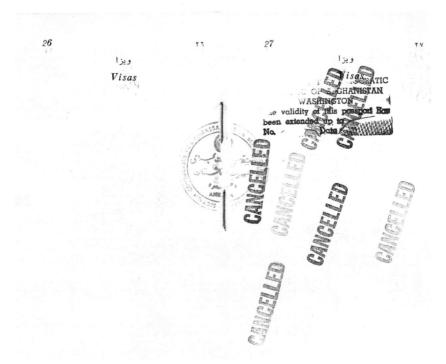

The page showing the cancellation of my passport

91

ویزا

Visas

ویزا

Visas

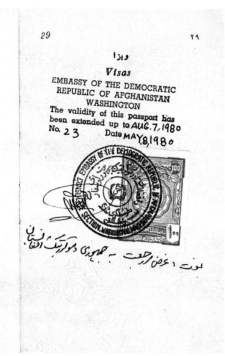

EMBASSY OF THE DEMOCRATIC
REPUBLIC OF AFGHANISTAN
WASHINGTON
The validity of this passport has
been extended up to AUG. 7, 1980
No. 2 3   Date MAY 8, 1980

Mr. Simkins was able to renew my passport

CHAPTER SIX

MY AMERICAN FAMILY

It was reinforcing the relationship, acceptance, and bond that developed between the Simkins family and myself. This was revealing in the introduction of one of Mr. Simkins letters about my immersion into his family, he writes, "In the comfort and safety of my home, I look across the room to the photographs of two handsome teenagers, grandchildren of my extended family. They have inherited the coloring and facial features typical of people from the Middle East. Their Afghani father is a naturalized American citizen, and successful entrepreneur. His story began almost forty years ago half way around the world."

When I came to America in late fall 1975 on a visa, I felt like a king. My American parents brought me to a store that had everything, and had it in abundance. I began an immediate love affair with America. I could not believe its potential, abundance, and freedoms. Never before in my life had I experienced such a thing. What was disconcerting to me is that I was only visiting America on a limited visa. After my American experience I could not even consider going back to Afghanistan where I was still a citizen. I dared not think about having to return. My American brother George was married the same year so I was able to attend his wedding.

When I arrived at my American parent's home in the United States I was given the guest room to sleep in and was touted as a special guest of honor. I had never been treated so well. Having survived the events in Lebanon, my family and I had formed a tight bond. I came into the lives of my American family at a time of crucial need. Without my efforts their struggles and survival would have been magnified or even hopeless.

With all the stress and uncertainty, and concerns I had, not only for my own wellbeing but for my new American family, when I came to the Simkins home all I did was sleep for the first month I was there. I would only get up to eat. The sleepless nights, the endless weapons fire, bombs, rockets, the constant uncertainty and roadblocks, had taken their toll. When I found myself in a safe environment my body needed to catch up. My American parents were concerned about me, they thought I was sick.

After about six months of having the guest room, my heroic status was downgraded to the basement with the other boys of the family. This was reinforcement to me however, that I was now fully part of the family. Besides, to me the basement was still like a castle. As I blended into the family I experienced sibling rivalry, usually over which television set and program to watch. The Simkins had one black and white television, and one color. Obviously the color set was the one everyone wanted to watch their programs on. My siblings treated me as one of them, complete with the bantering and sibling rivalry that you see in any other family.

It was interesting being immersed in another culture to experience how things were done differently. To see people that did not have to endure the daily burdens of just surviving, where most things were still done by hand and took the majority of the day to do. I knew the reality of growing up in a culture that suppressed me. A culture that did not give opportunities or hope. I felt so lucky. I had made it to America, something that had not even been a dream since I never thought it possible.

It was easy to see the potential and opportunities here in the greatest free country ever. I noticed that most Americans born into this society took it for granted. But for someone who has experienced a suppressed society, it is like you have been stumbling around in the dark and then suddenly there is this bright light freeing you.

I have always looked at things positively and have been lucky to have kept up my health and hope. And I have always liked people and interacting with them. There was always a rainbow to chase, and I always had an ambition to better myself and work hard to accomplish my goals. This drive I see in other immigrants to this great country. They come to America for its opportunities and freedoms. They come to better their lives and secure their future, and are willing to work hard to do so.

Coming from a country like Afghanistan where people were judged by their ethnic differences, and subsequently, in Lebanon where the two greatest divisions were divided down religious lines, i.e. whether you were Christian or Muslim, I did not give much attention to politics or political parties. There were political parties in Afghanistan as well as Lebanon, and in the other nations I had visited, but at the time I was only trying to survive and make "ends meet," as they say.

When I came to America it was different. There were many cultures and religions, all of them coexisted peacefully with each other. On occasion I would hear discussions between my American parents about political and social issues. At the time Gerald Ford was President of the United States, with a Presidential election only a year away. I learned that my American mother, Mrs. Simkins was a Democrat, and that my American father Mr. Simkins, was a Republican. I learned that these were the two predominant parties in the United States. There were other lesser parties but they did not have the following.

Therefore, my first real education in American politics occurred in the Simkins household. This became more obvious when Mary Louise was elated when Jimmy Carter beat President Ford in the ensuing presidential election. The election had been a learning experience for me. There was a difference of opinion between the two Simkins on the candidates.

I came from a nation which at the time was a monarchy. Under a monarchy there is only the will of the ruler, therefore, party affiliation is not viable. In this type of political environment the roots of choice through a party or its affiliation cannot take seed. As I said, there were political parties in Lebanon and other Arab nations in which I traveled, but I had never concerned myself with parties until I came to America.

I learned that Americans as a people can have differences, and different beliefs but still coexist peacefully. That did not happen in my native land, where one predominant group persecuted the other. The Pashtuns considered my culture, the Hazara as lesser than all others and treated us as such. Ironically, both of our groups were of the same religion but different sects, to them it did not matter.

I also learned that in America as a citizen you had a vote because America was a democracy. I grew up in a monarchy. I learned that America had a Constitution to guarantee our freedoms as citizens and individuals. In addition to this, the designers of our government they call the Founding Fathers, gave us additional protection with a Bill of Rights. The United States of America declared itself a Constitutional Republic.

America became strong because it was built on individual aspirations, strengths, endeavors and hard work. A collective individual initiative built productive farms, grew cities, and improved our quality of life through economy, education, a strong judiciary, and a standing army to protect our nation. Given these guarantees, America grew to a world power. It was a success story that grew from colonies to world leader.

What concerns me is that since I was able to come to the United States, America has become polarized. Parties have changed their focus and principles. This has created a great divide in our society. It is as though we are in a social civil conflict, ideology verses ideology. This divide is not good for America. The decades that I have been in America I have seen this steadily change.

It has always been our individual initiative that has made us strong, and a world leader. This same power in each of us as Americans is what will help us overcome our current challenges, to continue our freedoms and leadership of the free world, and freadoms for all future generations of Americans to enjoy.

We have always been a strong and morally guided people, we must continue to uphold the principles instilled in us by our Founding Fathers over two centuries ago. We must be involved as citizens.

.   .   .

Dr. Charles Simkins, my American father, was also my role model, which I never had in my natural father. Originally from the state of Kansas. Charles was the typical American child and high school student of that pre World War Two era. He lettered in basketball and baseball. From high school he went into the military and then what they used to call a, "Teachers College." At the time there was only a two year degree required to teach in public school.

When World War Two broke out Charles was eighteen years old. Like most people his age during that time he was eager to serve his country. He took a train to a nearby town to enlist in the Marine Corps, this was two days after Pearle Harbor was bombed. The recruiters did not contact him until the following summer, however. Impatient Charles enlisted in the Kansas National Guard in the meantime. When he was finally contacted by the Marine Recruiting, he had to be honorably discharged from the Kansas National Guard.

Charles was sent to Bowling Green, Ohio for training. He was a classmate of Eva Marie Saint, who later became an award winning actress. At the time the military put many of its officer candidates in what was called the V-12 program, where they were sent to a university for some of their training, then on to "boot camp" at Parris Island, South Carolina. After the completion of his training, Charles was commissioned a Second Lieutenant and stationed before going overseas in Camp Lejeune, North Carolina.

After he was settled at the camp, Mary Louise came to Camp Lejeune to be married to Charles. Years later Mr. Simkins would quip that he, "Married the farmer's daughter." Charles served three and a half years with the Marines in World War Two. After the war, the Simkins returned to Kansas to go to college. Charles also joined the military reserve.

Charles attended Kansas State College where he obtained double majors in Agriculture and Social Science. After graduation he was hired at the college as a soil instructor for two years. From this beginning in Agricultural Science, Charles got the opportunity to work on an experimental station at the University of Idaho for improving potatoes. He worked three years on this project. Charles then returned to Kansas State to pursue his Master's degree, and then into a doctorate program for a year. After receiving his doctorate, he was hired by the University of Minnesota to teach at their agriculture campus in Saint Paul. His job involved teaching and travel to various sites throughout Minnesota.

While teaching at the University of Minnesota, Mr. Simkins was hired by the Tennessee Valley Authority to educate and train growers in Iran to raise wheat and rice. This assignment was for five years. The goal usually for these assignments was to increase yields by teaching local farmers good practices. Mr. Simkins also had a two year assignment in Cyprus during their civil war.

After this assignment Mr. Simkins went to work for the United Nations in their Food and Agriculture Organization (FAO). Most FAO assignments were for five years. He was then contacted by the dean of the University of Minnesota, and accepted an assignment in Chile where he was involved with improving livestock and crops. Mr. Simkins taught at the Catholic University in Santiago, he quipped that his title was, "Jefe de la fiesta", chief of the party.

This project had sponsorship through the Rockefeller Foundation. Considering all the countries Mr. Simkins had lived in during his career, when asked which his favorite was, he replied, "Chile was my favorite", and added that the women were also very beautiful in Chile. From Chile Mr. Simkins returned to the University of Minnesota to teach and do extension work for a year.

The United Nations program manager then asked Mr. Simkins if he would go to Lebanon, where he initially came in 1974 to setup. As the reader is aware, Lebanon became a challenging assignment for Mr. Simkins and his family, and where a good portion of this writing takes place. After Lebanon Mr. Simkins spent two years at the United States Agency for International Development (USAID) in Washington D.C. There he was chief of the Soil and Water division. The USAID's goal was to provide development and humanitarian assistance around the world. (See Definitions in the Appendix) In year 2010 the greatest portion of the USAID's budget was utilized in my native country. Afghanistan received $2.75 billion dollars from the USAID that year.

As mentioned earlier most of Mr. Simkins assignments were for five years. When abroad on an assignment the United Nations would give a leave to come home every two years, and would ship items home. When Mr. Simkins was in Lebanon he was able to come home during the winter and teach at the University of Minnesota. Mr. Simkins assignments required him to fly all over the world.

On April 4, 1979 Mr. Simkins was on the last leg of a routine flight which began in Saudi Arabia. It became the infamous Trans World Airlines Flight 841 from New York to Minneapolis/ Saint Paul International Airport, and made national headlines for several days. As the plane was cruising at 39,000 feet over Saginaw, Michigan it began a sharp roll to the right. The autopilot and pilot were unable to compensate for the sudden roll and the plane went into a spiral dive. Within sixty-three seconds it lost 34,000 feet and did two complete rolls. The pilot did not gain control of the plane until it had dropped to only five thousand feet. By extending the landing gear the pilot was able to slow the aircraft and regain control. Mr. Simkins remembers feeling a big bump when this occurred. The incident became known as, "The plane that fell out of the sky."

The near catastrophe was caused by a front maneuverable surface called a slat, on the right wing used in landing. The plane made an emergency landing at the Detroit Metropolitan Airport. Hoot Gibson, the pilot, was an overnight national hero. There were eighty-two passengers on board, with only eight injured. Mr. Simkins remembers there was a group of children on board who were being adopted from India. When the plane dropped all the children hit the roof of the cabin. The airline arranged a settlement with the passengers, which amounted to $50,000 dollars each. Mr. Simkins was never part of the settlement because he was off on another assignment.

After the plane finally landed safely, many of the passengers would not fly to their final destination, but instead opted for transportation by bus. It had been too heralding of an experience for them. Years after surviving Flight 841, when asked about flying again after his experience, Mr. Simkins nonchalantly replied, "I did not fly for a while." When he did fly and mentioned he was on the infamous Flight 841, the airline would immediately upgrade him to First Class. The rest of his life he preferred driving to flying. The incident was later made into a movie.

After Lebanon, Mr. Simkins' accepted an assignment in Burma, then Uganda both five years each. The last assignment through a government agency or college was in Uganda. The project in Uganda was supported by the Ohio University Research Institute, originally built by the British. Mr. Simkins accepted other assignments after Uganda but only as a consultant.

One of his consulting jobs was in China. This assignment was near China's northern border with Russia. China wanted to grow grapes and begin a wine industry. Both grapes and wine would be good export products. In the northern area there was plenty of land to support vineyards, and a winery. Climate conditions were conducive to growing grapes, and there was no shortage of manpower. Mr. Simkins remembers there were greenhouses filled with grape cuttings from the United States.

The Chinese government gave Mr. Simkins team a small detachment of Red Army guards that would accompany them and see to their entertainment and well being. In the evenings they would all socialize over dinner and drinks. Mr. Simkins, an ex Marine and in his later life, found it amusing that he was able to, "Drink the young Red Army guards under the table."

Another time Mr. Simkins consulted in Hungary to obtain the highest yields and expansion on popcorn. The person who perfected microwave popcorn, so it could be stored at room temperature, James Watkins introduced his brand of microwave popcorn called ACT II. He contacted Mr. Simkins to consult in

Hungary where he had established resources to grow popcorn to supply his demands. Mr. Watkins wished to increase yields and improve qualities needed for the best popcorn. To be an effective popcorn kernel, it needs to expand to many times its size. One of the better popping kernels expands thirty-two times. For his lifelong service and accomplishments, Mr. Simkins received an Honorary Degree from Kansas State University as an outstanding alumnus.

Mary Louise Simkins, Dr. Simkins' wife was his complement. She was short, Irish, and feisty. Whenever someone would address her as only Mary, she would correct them by saying, "Excuse me, my name is Mary Louise." Once corrected you did not make the same mistake twice. Mrs. Simkins had a lot of energy and was a most giving person. She would volunteer with charitable organizations when at home in the United States, and would volunteer to teach when abroad.

When I came to America, the Simkins had me attend Grace High School, an Archdiocesan co-educational Catholic High School. Mrs. Simkins would help me with my homework. I was immersed in a totally different language, culture and curriculum. I even had to train myself to write in the opposite manner than Arabic. In Arabic you write from the right to the left, the opposite we do in the western world. This alone was like learning to drive on the opposite side of the street. You had to retrain your mind. Mary Louise would not let me speak my native language. She made me use only English. She would get upset with Mr. Simkins when he would sometimes speak to me in Arabic.

At the time the school I attended was called Grace High School. When the successful Totino pizza family contributed to the school it was renamed Totino-Grace High School. Rose and Jim Totino originally opened their Pizza takeout restaurant in 1951 and it became an instant success. By 1962 the family built a frozen pizza plant to keep up with the demand. In 1975 they sold to Pillsbury Corporation which later became part of the General Mills family of food products. Rose Totino became vice-president, the first female to become an executive in their corporate history.

Mary Louise would help me with my studies three or four hours each night. She was a patient teacher and person. Then she would be up cooking me breakfast at five AM the next morning to give me a good send off to my classes. She was very dedicated to the success of others, and took me in as her own child. Whenever I would be late, or miss dinner I would call to let her know. And if I would come home late even though I was in my twenties at the time, she would be up waiting for me.

When she did not agree with one of her children's comments or actions, or when upset with anyone, she would give them, "her eye." It was usually all that was needed the message got across and was effective. During my first year in the United States Mary Louise took me everywhere with her. We delivered Meals on Wheels, I would help her carry in the meals, and we would do community charity work together. She was very community involved and active in her church. She always kept busy.

Mary Louise was very family orientated and caring. Just about every evening for dinner she would have extra people over. She always had her children's friends come to eat with us. Coming from my early background this was a great reinforcement and experience for me. Even though I had always had a positive outlook, believing that things would always get better and workout, to see how a family could live with the caring and nurturing that was given to me, was inspiring.

When I graduated from Grace High School it was one of the proudest moments for me and for my American family, but most especially for Mary Louise. All her efforts, caring and nurturing had come to fruition. It was mostly through her efforts, and her prodding that, "I know you can do it," I was able to graduate. She would help me late into the evening to get through my lessons for the next day, sometimes catching herself nodding off.

Even after I got my first house, I was expected to not be late for dinner, Mary Louise would say, "Joe is going to be here." She was very helpful when I moved into my first apartment and stocked up my refrigerator. From there on whenever she would leave the country, she would see to it that my refrigerator was well stocked.

I was thirty-four years old in 1990 when I got my citizenship. It was one of the proudest moments for me and my American family. Mr. and Mrs. Simkins were in Africa, but my brother John the artist and photographer, took pictures of the ceremony. There were over forty people from around the world that received their citizenship on that day. After I received my citizenship, I ran up and down the street with an American flag. My sibling was surprised by my actions, and a little embarrassed that I was carrying on so.

As I have mentioned, Mary Louise's dedication to her fellow human beings brought her all over the world where Mr. Simkins was on assignment. She would teach, assist in humanitarian aid, or help the local peoples in any way. She was a complement to her husband's mission in this way.

I remember the last time we were together. I brought her to the airport, she was going to join Mr. Simkins in Uganda, his latest assignment. We were driving south on Snelling Avenue in Saint Paul, we were talking and just before a street called Larpenteur we collided with another vehicle, which only damaged fenders. We arrived at the airport and as I was unloading her luggage she started crying. When I asked her what was troubling her she said she was just having a hard time leaving home this time.

I asked her why she had to go, why couldn't she just stay home this time? I reinforced to her that she could stay, that she did not need to go. Her response was, "The kids over there need me, we are building a church and it needs a roof." Mr. Simkins assignment in Uganda lasted from 1989 to 1994. This was one of his last assignments through a government agency. Given the apprehension and insecure feeling of Mrs. Simkins, who was normally a strong person; and the fact we had had an accident that day, it was as if fate was speaking to us.

That was the last time I saw my adopted American mother, who had helped me so much and brought me into her family as one of her own. That last meeting will always bring tears to my eyes, had I only known I would have insisted that she not go. It was as if fate was trying to warn her, but was unable to override her giving and caring nature to be able to change her destiny. In a quizzical way, I even wished the vehicle accident would have been more involved so that she would have had to stay in American.

After Mary Louise had been in Uganda for several years, one day she felt ill. She had a fever and thought she had the flu. She would accompany Catholic sisters to various locations and help them. The next morning the sisters found Mary Louise in a coma. The sisters at the monastery took care of her until Mr. Simkins, who was away in the field, returned. Mary Louis never came out of her coma and died of complications due to malaria.

Mary Louis Simkins is pictured on the front cover of this book, posing on the camel I hold steady, in front of the antique store.

My American father and myself during the writing of this book

CHAPTER SEVEN

MY RE-LIFE

I am so fortunate to be an American. When I was struggling in Afghanistan and working in Middle East nations, I never thought it possible that I would ever be free to do what I wanted. To be able to make my own decisions, have opportunity and live a free life. That is what I am able to do in America. I do not know what I would do if I could no longer enjoy the opportunities that my new country has given me. As I have written earlier, I love the United States of America.

My children will have opportunity and a good education. They did not have to endure the hardships and experiences I endured. I did not know from day to day how I would be treated, what could happen to me, and what opportunity, if any, I would have as a Hazara in my former country. All that changed when I became an American citizen. I was assured of my safety, opportunity, and personal freedom.

At the writing of this book, I have been in the United States for over three decades. I have enjoyed a good life and have been successful. That is what happens in America. If you are willing to work hard, you will accomplish a lot. The opportunities are there, you must only accept them and be willing to put forth the effort, and have the desire to succeed. This I have done. That is why I wanted to tell my story. To share with those others who have spent all their lives here in the United States, or to those who have just immigrated to America. The opportunity is there for all.

The world over, people want to live in freedom but they are born into the environment they are given. If they have not experienced anything different, they may not really understand what true freedom is, or how to obtain it. That was me as a child until I learned about Iran, and how it had a large ethnic population which was the same as mine. This was my first thought of how to make my life better, how to have a life that would give me less persecution and greater choices and freedom.

I was lucky. I was able to accomplish my goal; freedom became a reality for me when I was able to come to the United States. I was fortunate, so many of my countrymen were not, they had to live the life they were given and be satisfied with it, knowing they had no other option. There are so many other Hazara, and peoples throughout the world, that would desperately like to change their environment. So they too can live their lives without disparity, discrimination, intimidation, or fear for their life on a daily basis. They are born into their reality, and their only resolution is that they have not known any better, therefore they accept it.

The future of the Hazara peoples and Afghanistan itself will depend directly on how the nation will function with the post presence of the American mission. My former nation can move forward only if it does not digress to its historic ethnic divide and disparity. War has devastated the Afghan people for decades. There has been a succeeding history of conquerors, war lords, and civil and political strife in Afghanistan's evolution. The Soviets invaded in 1979. After their defeat Afghanistan was launched into a civil war in the 1990s, and then the Taliban came and they were eventually suppressed by the United States military. At the crossroads of ancient trade routes, Afghanistan is not new to foreign presence or occupation.

The United States mission after containing the Taliban brought stability to the area. This has given a window of opportunity to the Hazara, and other subjugated groups within Afghanistan. However, the future is in question. Will Afghanistan be able to heal its ethnic differences to find common ground so peace can work? Will the Taliban reemerge as a force to be reckoned with again? Will the absence of a stabilizing force launch Afghanistan into another civil war? The answers to these questions will determine Afghanistan's future.

This is a pivotal time for my former nation. It is at the threshold of accepting democracy and is happening at a time when great strides could be made to move it forward. There are indicators that things are improving, but one must always be skeptical given Afghanistan's long history and tradition of wars, unrest, and ethnic differences. Can Afghanistan overcome its previous customs and ethnic differences? Can it continue to function as a democratic form of government? Only time will tell.

A good summary was given on Afghanistan's Web Site (*www.afghanistans.com*) titled: *"When you think Afghanistan Imagine"*

"Where 20 years of war has totally crippled the economy, and you must try to somehow survive day-by-day by scrounging enough food to feed your children. Where people do not have the facilities to receive an education. Where people do not have the facilities to receive treatment at hospitals. Where, on average, men die at 40 years of age and women 43. Where hundreds of thousands of people are maimed, disabled, or blind because of war and land mines. Where you face a high chance of becoming blind or crippled because of the lack of fresh fruit and vegetables, causing vitamin deficiency. If you are blind or crippled, no one can help you because those that are not blind or crippled need help as well."

I hope this book will help the reader understand how other cultures and peoples must live even today. There are few areas on earth that enjoy the freedoms we take for granted in the United States. The story I have told is how I struggled and the hardships I experienced, to get to where I am today. Hopefully other than being entertaining, this writing will also enlighten and encourage the same in others. There is still plenty of opportunity in America if someone is willing to work hard.

If you speak with anyone around the world, each of us is the same. We all wish for peace, freedom, opportunity, and safety to live and raise our families. It's been called the "American dream," and is the reason why so many people from around the world have come to the United States. America never had a colonial history, the areas our military have been sent to during our two hundred year history have never been occupied for long, or set up as a colony. We have only tried to institute democratic government with free elections. This has been our history.

In writing this book I have had to revisit those areas of my mind that I have closed off for years. Many events in my earlier life were painful to relive. During the writing I had periodic dreams and nightmares about events and incidents that I had chosen to lock away. One day one of my children frantically awoke me because I was pleading, "Don't take me, don't take me..." I was dreaming that I was being captured. I have had to open these areas and events to tell my full story. In the long run this will be good therapy for me, to have once again revisited these memories, so I can permanently put them to rest.

There is a growing Hazara community in Colorado and other areas of the United States. Colorado is a state with geography and climate similar to that from which the Hazara came. They are a close community and readily help new arrivals with housing, jobs, and transportation. They have been able to realize the American dream and the opportunities that are still in America. They are a peaceful and industrious community. In recent years they have organized themselves and have made their voice heard to help their fellow Hazara in Afghanistan.

The Hazara community post articles and maintain web pages all devoted to the atrocities and mistreatment of the Hazara peoples in Afghanistan. Their proactive stance is helping to make people, the world over, aware of the mistreatment and persecution of their brethren in Afghanistan. I find that the Hazara have adapted well to their new America home. They have blended into the community and have become a respected part of the society. They treasure the freedoms they experience here.

I have become acquainted with many people from the Middle East and from my native Afghanistan since living in the United States. One acquaintance is a physician and surgeon from Afghanistan. Doctor Sajady has his own interesting story of how he came to the United States by the invitation of US President Eisenhower. He became a surgeon. But because he was not Pashtun, who filled most positions of prominence, he was relegated to treat inmates of prisons. One of the Pashtun doctors who had worked with Dr. Sajady said to a fellow physician, "He's a good surgeon, too bad he is Shi'a."

Dr. Sajady became the head of the American hospital in Afghanistan in the 1960s. In 1961 a physician consultant to US President Eisenhower, Dr. Paul Dudley White told him that, "It's smelling Russian" referring to the increasing influence of the communist Soviet Union (USSR) in Afghanistan and the overall region. One day Dr. White asked Dr. Sajady to go to lunch with him. Lunch was at the American embassy, and Dr. Sajady was given a letter to give to customs, that he was a guest of the President of the United States.

Dr. Sajady took the opportunity and came to the United States. He was a guest of Dr. White when he came to America. Dr. Sajady eventually came to the University of Minnesota and settled. After decades of running a successful practice, in 2001 he retired and converted his practice to a nonprofit free clinic, and continued to donate his time and services to the community.

Another friend was a freedom fighter when the Russians invaded Afghanistan. He escaped over the mountains in 1980 to find an interim opportunity in Germany. There he attended four years in High School to learn German. He was eventually able to immigrate to the United States in 1984, where he had to attend High School again in his mid-twenties to learn English. He ultimately earned an engineering degree. The love of freedom is inherent in each human being, and each of us will struggle and risk a lot to obtain it.

When I came to America, my ambition and focus to get ahead and do well for myself, was almost epidemic. As I have mentioned I came to the United States the first time in November 1975 with a tourist Visa. Mrs. Simkins enrolled me in Grace High School which I attended for two months. I returned to Damascus in April 1976 then came back to the United States in September 1976 and attended Grace High School again. I was nineteen years old at the time, and graduated in 1978. The following year I enrolled in an Area Vocational Technical Institute into an eighteen month auto mechanics course. I graduated in 1980.

I am self-educated in many ways and have always learned quickly. That is why I have picked up other languages so well. I learned much from my American father. He was from what they now call the Great Generation. This was the generation that faced one of the greatest wars in history when they were only in their teens and early twenties. They readily went to war to fight for the country they loved. After they won the war they returned to build one of the biggest economies in history while raising the next generation. This Greatest Generation maintained their principles, way of life, responsibility, and their faith, to build the great society. They gave more back than what they took.

Dr. Charles Simkins would be up at five o'clock in the morning every day. A neighbor once quipped that if everyone was up as early as Mr. Simkins, there would have been less of a future Baby Boomer generation.

I took the principles of my American father's generation, I used them to develop and structure my own philosophy. I have always had a good work ethic, it is what has got me through life and made me a successful person. Then, coming to America allowed me to utilize my skills to progress and grow. In America you only need the desire to be successful. A sign I continue to display as a reminder to this is, "Winners never quit, and quitters never win." That has always been my philosophy.

I gain insight and motivation from these messages. They give me daily direction and focus. Dr. Wayne W. Dyer is a motivational speaker and writer that I follow who has been an influence to me. His message is simple; through self-development, "...it is possible for every person to live an extraordinary life." All persons at times need inspiration, refocus, and reminder of purpose; it is all part of our human experience.

Although I did not see auto mechanics as my lifelong goal it was a trade I could always fall back on. I had to continue going to school while I was in the United States. Even though I had gone through high school at Grace High School, I was still trying to be comfortable with my new culture. Learning the language was an ongoing endeavor itself, compounded by daily auto mechanics classes, I was kept busy.

I was treated with respect by most Americans. People would readily help me and befriend me, they acknowledged no differences. Only on occasion would I be approached by someone with reservation. Some people were reserved around me because I spoke a little different as I was learning to be fluent in English. There were few times that I actually felt what could be called discrimination. This occurred at the school I attended to learn auto mechanics.

One of the auto mechanics instructors was older and seemed disappointed by life in general. The school knew enough to not put any but traditional white male students with him. He did not appear to be a happy person, and found me especially as a target of his frustrations. I was not put in his class, but students and instructors worked together in the shop area. He bullied me in front of others, swore at me, and called me "Geek." He had a poor tone to others as well, but most to me. I would plead with him not to pick on me.

At times I would hear other students complain about the same instructor. There were other ethnic cultures going through the course that were supported through various programs through the government. The instructor would refer to them as, "free loaders" and other students would sometimes allude to them as, "getting a free ride." My American parents were helping me get through school.

Being a student with such an instructor was an education to me. Everything up until this daily interaction had been a rewarding experience for me in America. My thoughts reverted to the monarchies I had traveled and worked in. I surmised that the instructor was a dictator, and he was getting away with it. I had experienced no discrimination at my High School. But when I came to the technical college, within two weeks the instructor was picking on me. This bothered me and made my days long and challenging.

I asked my American mother why this was happening, but she only blew it off. She told me in essence to deal with it, that the course was short and that the instructor would retire someday. That is how her generation, and the generations before her, would deal with these problems. They treated them on an individual basis. They believed that you should face your problems and deal with them, which would make you a stronger, better person. The message I got from Mrs. Simkins was, "That's the way it is." I only confided in my American mother, not my father at this time, I knew he would have had a different opinion.

I dealt with the innuendos and name calling until an incident that occurred just three days prior to my graduation. I was working on my dad's Buick in one of the stalls during the end of a class changeover. The stalls were utilized between first and second year student sessions. Second year students would utilize the stalls to work on their vehicles beginning at seven o'clock in the morning. Then first year students would work on their vehicles beginning at one o'clock in the afternoon when their session began. The Buick happened to be in the instructor's stall that was needed for the next session. It was in the stall of the instructor that spent the last eighteen months, "riding me."

Mr. Simkins' Buick was not starting. I was frustrated because the car would not start no matter what I tried. The instructor began pacing back and forth impatiently waiting for his stall while calling me names. He continued this as I was frantically working to get the car started. He physically pushed me and tapped the hood of the car at each pace to show that he was irritated. The third time he nudged me the hood fell on my head. I was already upset because the car would not start, I knew I was holding up the next class from getting started, and I had to rely on the Buick to get me to a painting job. When the hood hit my head it set me off, my instinctive involuntary reflex training reacted and I punched him in the face. He was dazed and then went down.

The other instructors came and helped with the changeover and situation. I went upstairs to the administer of the mechanics shop to explain my side of the incident. Then I left. The next day the instructor whom I had punched apologized to me and pleaded with me not to register a complaint, in his own words to not, "turn him in." Ironically, another instructor who taught engines took me out to lunch and thanked me for what I had done. The other instructors found him intolerable as well. After graduation I told my American father about the incident with the instructor at my school. As an ex Marine I already knew what his solution would have been, in his own words, had he known about the incident at the time he would have, "Beat the crap out of him!" The incidences I experienced while in trade school are rare in today's world.

Despite my frustrations with the auto mechanics teacher, my entrepreneurial spirit festered in me. I did not let my lack of citizenship quell my drive to get ahead. Although I was in the United States on a student visa, which limited me from working, I began repairing people's automobiles. One time I had six vehicles in one state of repair or another in my parent's front driveway. This prompted my American mother to "suggest" to me that they be moved so the rest of the family could come and go, and be able to park their vehicles. My adopted mother did not have to ask anyone twice to have something done. Despite her short stature, she wielded a lot of respect.

I would never turn down an opportunity. While living with the Simkins, Mary Louise offered her eldest son John who was an artist, an opportunity to paint the outside of their house. She offered him four dollars and fifty cents an hour knowing he had the experience. It was a reasonable wage for such a job at the time. If John was not interested she would offer me the opportunity, but because of my lack of experience (I had never painted before) she offered me only two dollars and fifty cents an hour instead. I was satisfied with the arrangement.

I prayed all night that John would not take the job so I could do it. Being on a student visa I was not able to work and needed money. Throughout the night I continued to calculate in my head the potential of money I could earn. The next day, my prayers were answered when John turned down the offer and I was given the opportunity to paint the exterior of the house. I took on the job with my usual energy and enthusiasm. Having never painted before, I learned as I worked. I painted the house, along with nearby bushes and structures, whose only fault was their proximity to the house. After I had finished, Mr. Simkins commented on my job saying that, "Everything was brown, including the steps." He never let me forget about the painted steps, which jokingly came up in conversations thereafter.

After this experience, my entrepreneurship took hold and I talked with neighbors about painting jobs. A neighbor and good friend of my American parents, who worked with me on projects and showed me how to fix things, hired me to paint his trim. From these first two paint jobs I launched a booming painting business and new career. I eventually even hired my American brother John. Who, as I already mentioned, had been given the initial opportunity to paint the Simkins house before me. My business thrived just on word of mouth.

One time when working on a job with my brother John, who was balkier than me, we carried a ladder with each of us at one end to our job site. In doing so, we passed in front of a house that was having a wedding reception. As we passed by carrying the ladder, one of the guests shouted out to the rest of the group, "Look! There's Laurel and Hardy." We could only share their laughter with them. After we had passed by the reception, I asked my America brother who Laurel and Hardy were. After he explained to me who they were, we both laughed.

To finish my jobs I would work many weekends, including Sundays. Mary Louise did not like me to work on Sundays. She considered Sunday to be enjoyed as a day of rest, and for family. I tried to respect her wishes, but my entrepreneurism tugged at me to complete my tasks and go on to the next, regardless of which day of the week it was. I wanted to get ahead. I wanted to earn money. That is why so many other people come to this country, to do better and be rewarded for their hard work.

It troubles me to see the changes that are occurring in the United

114

States today. We seem to be struggling among ourselves as Americans. Some want America to go in one direction, while others are concerned that the principles that we have enjoyed for over two hundred years are being eroded. This concerns me greatly since I have experienced non-free societies in my past, and never want to return to such an existence.

It surprises me when I hear people criticize America, and say that it has not done enough because we still have poor people. Poor in America does not equate to poor elsewhere. In America the poor have cars, radios, televisions, computers, and cell phones. I was raised truly poor. Poor in America means that you earn less than 34,000 dollars a year. When compared to what the average Afghan earns yearly, it helps you understand what it really means to be poor.

In America between charitable and religious organizations, and the government, the poor have ample resources. No one starves in America unless they have an addiction or mental challenge. In comparison growing up as a child in Afghanistan I only had a change of clothes once a year. We could not afford such luxuries even as a radio. Our life was that of subsistence, "If we worked we ate -- if we didn't work we died."

There is no comparison of how I lived as a child in Afghanistan and how American children grow up in America. Children in the Unites States grow up in front of a computer or television screen. They have electronic games and devices at their disposal. Children in America are overweight from lack of exercise and poor diets built around carbohydrates, especially in what we call, "fast foods." Autism, diabetes, and many other diseases are on the rise, and so is cigarette smoking. Futurists are already saying that the next generation may not live as long as the previous generation because of these poor habits and afflictions. They are warning the next generation that their habits and way of life will reduce their life expectancy.

We must not lose our principles or circumvent our Constitution. As an immigrant I had to learn about the Constitution. It is the greatest written document of freedom ever. In its few pages it outlines the rights and freedoms that we, as Americans, have been able to enjoy.

I readily share with everyone, the American system has given me choices and opportunities. As I mentioned, when I first came to the United States, I attended a Technical College in Auto Mechanics, but never did auto repair as a profession or business. I would at times have a second part-time job to supplement my income. One time I got a job as a bus boy at a Japanese restaurant, but only worked for two weeks. By then I had been an entrepreneur and when I received my paycheck for busing, it convinced me that having a second, hourly job, was not worth it. I would do better by pushing a little harder for one more client. It reinforced to me that it was more lucrative and beneficial to work for myself as an entrepreneur. I continued to build my painting business.

In November 1980, a friend asked me to accompany him on a trip to Arizona to deliver his parents automobile to them. On the way we made sure to stop in Las Vegas, where at one of the casinos I won on a card game and then quit.

While traveling in Phoenix we were hit when another driver ran a stop light. The driver did not have insurance. I was still relatively new to how everything worked in the United States, especially with how auto insurance worked. I did not know that I was covered by my own policy, and also that of my friend's who I was driving with. When brought to the hospital and asked if I had insurance I responded, "No." A doctor examined me in the emergency room and released me. I continued to have a headache and pain so I returned to the hospital the following morning.

After the accident, I attended a pain clinic when we returned to my home state. Under my insurance plan they would also retrain, and find a job for me because of the injury I could no longer paint. I was restricted to what I could lift, and put on pain medication. This became a pivotal time for me. I received treatment and attended the pain clinic for several months. It took me two years to return to my former self. I would still have discomfort at times due to the accident. I also had to be withdrawn from the pain medication to break my dependence on it.

The job counselor, who worked with me said that I would only be able to do factory work where I could sit down. They arranged for me to pick up an application from a local factory. The factory evidently needed employees because it currently had a strike. I had to go to a back entrance through the active strike to receive an application. The workers on strike shouted and swore at me as I crossed their picket line. After I had returned home, I asked my American mother why the employees on strike were so angry at me. She replied, "Because you want to take their job." I did not want to take anyone else's job.

I returned to the pain clinic the next day and explained to them what had happened. The counselor told me that if I did not take the job at the factory they had arranged for me, I would instead have to go on welfare. I had learned what welfare was. This hurt my feelings because I did not think I had to take the only job they had available for me, and that my only other option was welfare. My emotion took over, I grabbed the counselors tie and explained to him that, "Where I come from, if we work we eat, if we don't we die!" And I left.

After my experience I thought there had to be another solution. In job training we were taught how to scan the newspaper want ad section, and how to prepare for interviews. I would read the daily want ads in the newspaper. One day in 1982 I saw an ad that said, "Be your own boss make 10,000 a month. Total Image." It was a company that promoted a protein diet. I was excited about the ad and told my American parents and siblings. They thought I was crazy to actually consider an ad that would promise so much. I met with a representative of the company and begin to promote their product. Total Image began with a dietary product but expanded into soaps, lotions and shampoos.

Sometimes after a long day I would go to a restaurant for a late dinner. Never giving up on my options, I would ask waitresses, or women sitting near, "Do you ladies want to lose some weight?"

117

and showed them a brochure. I would get mixed reactions. Some pretended to be interested, while others just gave me a, "leave me alone look." My persistence paid off, however, because after about nine months I finally earned ten thousand dollars in one month. I had reached my goal, but unfortunately the company struggled and went out of business. It could only pay the remainder of what I was due in product when it dissolved in 1984.

One of the people I knew at Total Image was a teacher and coach who introduced me to Arthur L. Williams, the teacher was already working with the company as a supplement to his income. Williams was a self made billionaire who formed his own company in insurance. His company became the largest seller of life insurance in the United States. The company was one of the first to have weekly video conferencing on the company's private television broadcast system. Williams wrote the book *Common Sense* about basic economy and investing. Its straight forward easy to understand writing and charts made it a popular book. A. L. Williams was also a very religions person.

I joined A. L. Williams in 1984 and got my financial license in January 1985. Arthur "Art" Williams ran a tight ship, which was part of his success. He expected his agents to look, act, and be professional. He made these points in no uncertain terms. I heard him say one time when referring to men with pierced earrings, "If you have earrings, you should also have breasts, or don't let the door hit you on the way out." Another rule Mr. Williams had was that at conferences he would pay for spouses that attended but not for girlfriends. At one conference in New Orleans there were 30,000 agents.

I have always had high expectations and goals, and have pushed myself to achieve them. This I did at A. L. Williams; I accomplished every goal I had set for myself. I first became a regional vice president, and then ultimately achieved my goal to become the highest level in sales as National Sales Director. I had an impressive upward mobile career with A. L. Williams. As the National Sales Director I oversaw up to fifteen vice presidents, and divisional and regional sales directors. As National Sales Director I worked every day and night. I would travel a lot, sometimes I would be so tired that on driving trips I would pull over alongside the road and take a short nap.

A. L. Williams convention in Hawaii 1986

Arthur William's company transitioned into Primerica Financial Services in 1991. I continued with the new company, but with any sale or acquisition, or change in management team, the dynamics of the original company is usually changed. That is what I experienced at Primerica. I remained with the new company for two years. Given my position, when I left people thought that I was crazy. But it was no longer for me, and knew I had to move on. Arthur Williams was a charismatic leader and I learned a lot from him.

I have had some losses and not every deal was the best, but that is the nature of entrepreneurism and investment, and ultimate financial independence. I kept looking into opportunities and investments.

In my office at A. L. Williams

While still at Primerica, I invested as one of four partners in a company I learned about from a person I met at the restaurant I was helping turn around, as their financial services advisor. The man was a chemist who had discovered chemicals that would change color when in direct sunlight. When embedded into tee shirt fabric it would change color when exposed to the ultraviolet (UV) of sunlight. The company was Sunny Color. Its popularity exploded, it was not long before we had orders for thousands of shirts.

Because of the slow and intricate chemical process, it was difficult to keep up with demand. The process was difficult to automate, and in trying to do so we went through a lot of expensive chemicals and shirt stock. The shirts would splotch and bleed and we were forced to throw hundreds of them away. One kilogram of chemical cost over $200 dollars at the time.

A popular jean and sports clothes manufacturer and distributor became interested in our product, but we could not guarantee the process. Through connections, I was even able to promote my shirts in Rome where several persons were interested to "buy in" with exclusive rights to the product. Because of the uniqueness of the product distributors were scampering to obtain rights to it. I remember that "Mood Rings" were also popular at this time, where the heat from your body would change their color. My involvement with Sunny Color was only about a year.

While in Rome I also took the opportunity to visit with the former head of the FAO for who my American father worked and I drove to the Beirut airport in the middle of the Lebanese civil war.

Sunny Color Brochure

In 1994 I made the decision to leave Primerica to become an independent Financial Services Advisor. I would recruit and train agents that would sell under me. Networking was a key to my success. I gained clients and my business began to prosper. As a financial services provider I helped people and businesses with their finances.

A financial services advisor to be the most effective at what he or she does needs to stay educated on the needs of their client, and on the climate of the economy and market. I was part of the Baby Boomer generation and so were most of my clients. As the Baby Boomer generation gravitated to middle life, I followed their progression as a good business practice. I eventually went from financial service advisor to long term care insurance.

It humbles me to hear the positive comments I receive from others about my character. I enjoy life. Most people know that I am self made, honest, and that like many others, I have struggled but have overcome my struggles to become successful. Others describe me as always on the go, a good family man, and a down to earth person. I feel that these are just common sense traits that should be shared by all human beings. I have always believed in ongoing self improvement, and I am a firm believer that, "Positive works, negative does not." This is my philosophy of life.

I have many friends and aquaintenances. I center myself around people. It is people that makes everything happen on earth. Machines are programmed and run by people, government is run by people, businesses and corporations are run by people, and our education system is run by people. I learned early in my life that I interacted well with others. That is why I have always preferred sales. If you can help others to do better, or be more comfortable, or to struggle less, you have done your job. If you help others it will help you, like the old saying in America, "What goes around comes around." If you help someone it will come back to you in good fortune.

Few know of my earlier years growing up in Afghanistan, and the persecution I had to bear just because I was born of the Hazara culture in my homeland. Fewer yet, know of my many life threatening experiences that I had to bear just to survive. Where I came from, I had little hope of ever being free.

The experiences, from my early life has given me an appreciation of life, of my family, and my opportunities and accomplishments. Few days go by that I do not think how lucky I am. I center my life around my family and friends. I have purposely honored the wishes of my wife and the lives of my children, to keep them private. The world belongs to my children. I only wish to give them the support to prepare them to do their best.

Even though I am haunted at times by my past, this writing has made me revisit my past and allowed me to move on. Each of us carries our own history with us. By sharing my story it has made me more at peace with myself.

For anyone to analyze themselves is a difficult task. As I look back on my life, to my experiences, my early goals and aspirations, and challenges, I have matured and so have my goals, ambitions, and philosophies. I did things in my early life that were dangerous and risky, and at the time I did not think twice about them. That power of youth, where you experience the moment with vigor and infallibility, has been replaced with life experience and maturity. I am more careful now about the decisions I make, and draw more on my experience. My youngest American sister who was a preadolescent girl at the time experiencing all these events, once said to me decades later, "You were crazy to do all the things you did." But I had a mission that drove me.

My goals and aspirations, the main focus of my earlier life, have given to family values, nurturing my children, and facing my mature years with the same positive approach I have always utilized in my life. I have a nice home in a good community, my children are receiving a good education, and I am preparing for my future years. These are the results of my hard work, ambition, and endless drive to get ahead. I need these reinforcements and reminders of my successes and accomplishments, just as I have always looked to motivational sayings for inspiration throughout my life.

This book acquaints the reader to a different part of the world, to different cultures and events, and to the struggles I had to endure to be able to become a citizen of one of the greatest nations on earth. In America I became a husband, father, and successful entrepreneur.

Waving at tourists and passersby atop our camel at the antique store in Lebonon

CHAPTER EIGHT

MY WISH: A FOUNDATION

A goal of mine is to setup a foundation for the benefit of Hazara women and children. Especially women and girls because of the hard, but short lives they experience. I wish to give them hope, opportunity, and a future. They need better healthcare, trained midwives, and good doctors and societal support. My mother died while giving birth.

I have always been concerned about the feelings, hopes, and well being of others. I draw those persons I befriend into my life and stay concerned about their well being. I was given hope when I met my American family. It was this contact that opened doors for me. I do not wish to think about what would have happened to me if I would have had to stay in Afghanistan. With the Taliban coming into power, I would have most likely perished or at best, undergone grueling experiences that would never have allowed me to be the same person.

That is why I want to establish some form of foundation to help women and children. I want to give those Hazara children born into the slavery of a persecuting society, hope. They deserve an opportunity and a chance. With the American troops drawing down, and the ultimate plan of full scale removal of all soldiers, my people will again be persecuted. It is what has happened for centuries, and will continue unless concerned individuals, groups, and nations help to stop this genocide from continuing once and for all.

My people have suffered long enough with no one coming to their aid. I wish to help children that are living in the same scenario I was as a child in Afghanistan. One person can make a difference, and can help save an innocent child, whose only mistake was by fate, they were born to one place on earth rather than another. They were born where opportunities do not exist for them.

Child mortality remains high in Afghanistan and many kids live on the streets in Kabul. According to the Afghanistan Minister of Public Health, "One in ten children die before age five." Maternal Mortality in Afghanistan is the second highest at 1900 out of 100,000.[1] There needs to be more health programs available to women and children that educate them, and give them good care and medicine especially during pregnancy.

As I have mentioned, child mortality in Afghanistan for children under age five years old is the second highest in the world. According to the United Nations Development Program for Afghanistan, "Most deaths among children under the age of five years are caused from vaccine preventable infections."[2] These are caused by lack of clean water and poor sanitation. The Afghan government has strived to increase immunization of children.

Child mortality rates are twenty percent lower in urban than in rural areas of Afghanistan because of the availability of cleaner water, better refuse resources, and more ready medical care.

The Afghanistan government has targeted goals to reduce child mortality rates through education, immunization, and overall improvement of conditions. This will take time, and any civil disruption or war will delay it. There will continue to be a disparity among rural verse urban areas for quite some time in the foreseeable future.

As I have said, this is a crucial opportunity for the Hazara. The Hazara must position themself and establish a strong base of worldwide outreach via the internet and world organizations. The Hazara have never been allowed this opportunity before. Therefore, they must make the best of it while the US troops remain. Since 2001 there have been many Hazara related websites and organizations established for the causes of the Hazara people. These resources are letting the world know about their plight. (See Appendix, Suggested Sources for Additional Information)

I hope this book raises awareness of the Hazara people of Afghanistan and their circumstance, and through its writing will help improve the lives of the people, especially the women and children, of my former nation.

¹ www.usaid.gov
²www.undp.org.af

APPENDIX

HISTORY OF AFGHANISTAN

Archeological finds in and near Afghanistan prove there has been human inhabitation for thousands of years in the area. Afghanistan is near what has been called the "cradle of civilization," where some of the earliest civilizations occurred, between the Tigris and Euphrates Rivers. As the cross-roads of the Middle East and Asia, Afghanistan has had a host of conquerors throughout its history. This has had direct effect on its economy, governance, its peoples, and society.

In its eastern fringe position and crossroads advantage, Afghanistan benefitted from these early civilizations, but has also brought conquering armies to its soil. Afghanistan was just east of Mesopotamia. There is evidence of early domestication of animals especially at the foothills of the Hindu Kush Mountains. Afghanistan has always been a "Crossroads of Asia."

With the many empires and dynasties, the Persian Empire 550 BC to 330 BC, was plagued by tribal revolts from Afghans in southwest Afghanistan. Alexander the Great conquered Afghanistan, but was unable to fully subdue its people and experienced on-going revolts from Afghan tribes. Subsequent empires after Alexander the Great included portions of Afghanistan in their territory.

During the Kushan Empire 30 to 300 AD the large Buddhas were carved into the mountain side at Bamiam, Afghanistan. By 530 AD the Persians reassured their control over Afghanistan until the Arabs introduced Islam. Afghanistan has been an Islamic state ever since.

Warlords, dynasties, and periodic inclusion in empires prevailed in Afghanistan. There were settlements, but also nomadic groups herding animals on seasonal basis. Some independent kingdoms existed also during this time. Trade continued as an important connection to other areas.

Afghanistan became part of Genghis Khan's empire with campaigns from 1219 to 1221. Its influence lasted over one hundred years. Afghanistan continued to go through successions of ruling dynasties.

In 1273 Marco Polo from Italy traveled through Afghanistan on his way to China. He discovered the "Silk Route" which opened the east to the west.

Afghanistan began to slowly emerge as an individual entity and take control of its own destiny.

In 1709 to 1713 Mirwais Hotak an influential Afghan tribal chief gained independence at Kandahar after a successful revolution against the Persian Safavid Dynasty. During this time the Persian government sent two large armies to regain Kandahar Province but was defeated by the Afghans. In 1715 Mirwais died of natural causes and his brother Abdul Aziz inherited the throne until he was killed by Mahmud Hotaki, son of Mirwais.

By 1722 The Battle of Gulnabad occurred, led by Mahmud, the Afghan army captured the Safavid capital of Isfahan and Mahmud was declared Shah of Persia. In 1725 Mahmud was murdered by his cousin Ashraf, son of Abdul Aziz and succeeded him as Shah of Persia.

In 1729 the Battle of Damghan occurred with Afsharid forces led by Nadar Shah defeated Ashraf and his army, by 1738 Nader invaded Kandahar and restored the Abdali ethnic Pashtuns to political prominence. In 1747 Ahmed Shah Durrani of the Abdali Pashtun confederacy declared the establishment of an independent Afghanistan with its capital at Kandahar.

In 1809 Shuja Shah Durrani signed a treaty of alliance with the United Kingdom. And in 1826 Dost Mohammed Khan took the throne in Kabul and proclaimed himself Emir (1826 to 1839).

From 1839 to 1842 the first Anglo-Afghan War occurred, beginning in March of 1839 a British expeditionary force captured Quetta. In August King Shuja was reinstated to the throne. In November 1841 a mob killed the British envoy to Afghanistan, and in January

1842 the Massacre of Elphinstone's army occurred, where a retreating British force of sixteen thousand was massacred by the Afghans. In 1857 Afghanistan declared war on Persia, and Afghan forces recaptured Heart.

Dost Mohammed Khan returned as Emir of Afghanistan (1842 to 1863). A chief of the Hazara in Hazarajat was Mir Yazdan bakhsh of Kharzer. An influential Hazara in Behsud (modern Wardak Province) who controlled the Shibar and Hajikak passes into Bamian. He was a threat to Dost Mohammed Khan who imprisoned him in Kabul. Mir Yazdan bakhsh was able to escape and returned to Behsud to resume controlling the Bamian passes.

In June 1863 Dost Mohammed Khan died suddenly. His successor was his son Sher Ali Khan.

During 1878 to 1880 the second Anglo-Afghan War begins with the refusal of a British diplomatic mission by Afghanistan. This mission was prompted by the response to the Russians who sent an uninvited diplomatic mission to Kabul.

In May 1879 to prevent British occupation of a large part of the country, the Afghan government ceded much of its power to the United Kingdom in the Treaty of Gandamak. Under the treaty most of the British and Indian soldiers withdrew from Afghanistan, and Afghanistan was permitted to maintain its internal sovereignty, but ceded their nation's foreign relations to the British. In July 1880 Abdur Rahman Khan was recognized as Emir of Afghanistan.

From 1891 to 1893 Hazara wars occurred under Abdur Rahman Khan. In late 1893 Abdur Rahman Khan and British representative Mortimer Durand signed an agreement establishing the Durand Line.

In 1901 Habibullah Khan, son of Abdur Rahman became Emir of Afghanistan. In February 1909 Habibullah was assassinated, his son Amanullah Khan declared himself King of Afghanistan.

In May 1919 Amanullah led a surprise attack against the British causing the third Anglo-Afghan War from May to August 1919. Emir Amanullah Khan declares independence from British influence.

In 1929 Emir Amanullah was forced to abdicate in favor of Habibullah Kalakani due to a popular uprising, former General Muhammad Nadir Shah took control of Afghanistan. In November 1933 Nadir was assassinated and his son, Mohammed Zahir Shah proclaimed King.

In 1953 General Mohammed Daud becomes Prime Minister and turns to the Soviet Union for economic and military assistance. He also introduces social reforms.

In 1963 Mahammad Daud was forced to resign as Prime Minister, and in1964 a new constitution was ratified which instituted a democratic legislature. In January 1965 the Marxist People's Democratic Party of Afghanistan (PDPA) held its first congress.

In 1973 Mohammed Daud seizes power in a coup and declares a republic.

In April 1978 the Saur Revolution occurred where military units loyal to the PDPA assaulted the Afghan Presidential Palace killing President Muhammad Daud Khan and his family. In May the PDPA installed its leader Nur Muhammad Taraki as President of Afghanistan. In July the same year a rebellion against the new Afghan government began with an uprising in Nuristan Province. In December a treaty was signed permitting deployment of Soviet military at the Afghan government's request.

In September 1979 Taraki was murdered by supporters of Prime Minister Hafizullah Amin. In December fearing the collapse of the Amin regime, the Soviet army invaded Afghanistan beginning the war with Russia. Several days later in December, Soviet troops occupied major government, military, and media buildings in Kabul, including the Tajbeg Palace and executed Prime Minister Amin.

In 1980 Babrak Karmal becomes ruler backed by the Soviets. Afghani groups begin fighting Russian forces with weapons supplied by the United States, Pakistan, China, Iran, and Saudi Arabia.

In April 1988 the Soviet government signed the Geneva Accords which included a timetable for withdrawing their armed forces.

By February 1989 the last of the Soviet troops left the country but civil war began in Afghanistan. In April 1992 Afghan political parties signed the Peshwar Accord which created the Islamic State of Afghanistan and proclaimed Mojaddedi its interim President. Gulbuddin Hekmatyar's Hezbi Islami, with the support of neighboring Pakistan began a massive bombardment against the Islamic State in the Kabul capital.

By June 1992 as agreed upon in the Peshawar Accord, Jamiat-e Islami leader Burhanuddin Abbani took over as President. Civil war ensued. In January 1993, the Durand Line Treaty expired which was supposed to return all Afghan lands to Afghanistan, but Pakistan refuses.

In August 1994 the Taliban begins to form in a small village between Lashkar Gah and Kandahar. In January 1995 the Taliban with the support of Pakistan, initiated a military campaign against the Islamic State of Afghanistan and its capital Kabul.

By September 1996 civil war in Afghanistan begins. The forces of the Islamic State retreat to northern Afghanistan. The Taliban conquer Kabul and establish the Islamic Emirate of Afghanistan and force a new extreme form of Islam onto the people. President Muhammad Najibullah, who had been under United Nations protection in Kabul was tortured and executed by the Taliban forces.

In 1997 the Taliban controls over two-thirds of the country and is recognized as the legitimate rulers of Afghanistan by Pakistan and Saudi Arabia. In August 1998 the Taliban captured Mazar-e Sharif forcing Abdul Rashid Dostum to exile. That same month

Cruise missiles were fired by the US Navy into four militant training camps in the Islamic Emirate of Afghanistan.

In 1999 the United Nations imposes an air embargo and financial sanctions to pressure Afghanistan to hand over Osama bin Laden to the Americans.

In March 2001 the Taliban destroy the historic Buddhas of Bamian, Afghanistan. In September only two days before the 9/11 attack on the United States, Northern Alliance resistance leader Ahmad Shah Massoud was killed in a suicide bomb attack by two Arabs disguised as French news reporters. After the September 11 attack on the United States, President Bush demanded the Taliban government to turn over the mastermind of the 9/11 attack, Osama bin Laden, and to close all terrorist training camps in the country. Bushes' dictate was refused by the Taliban.

By October 2001 the United States and United Kingdom launched Operation Enduring Freedom against al-Qaeda and the Taliban with aerial bombing. The Northern Alliance forces enter Kabul. In early December the United Nations Security Council authorized the creation of the International Security Assistance Force (ISAF) to help maintain security in Afghanistan. By mid-December 2001 the United Nations Security Council, at its International Conference on Afghanistan in Germany, chose Hamid Karzai as head of the Afghan Interim Administration.

In July 2002 Hamid Karzai was appointed as President of the Afghan transitional administration. In December the same year another grand assembly was held to consider a new Afghan constitution. In August 2003 NATO oversees security in Kabul. Ironically, it is the first commitment NATO has done outside of Europe.

In October 2004 Hamid Karzai, the interim president, was elected President of the Islamic Republic of Afghanistan, the first democratically elected president of Afghanistan. In 2005 A Taliban insurgency began after a Pakistani decision to station eighty thousand soldiers near the Durand Line border with Afghanistan.

In March 2006 US President Bush visited Afghanistan to inaugurate the renovated US Embassy in Kabul. In October of the same year NATO assumes security for all of Afghanistan. In May 2007 border skirmishes began between Pakistan and Afghanistan.

In August 2007 it is reported by the UN that opium production had risen to record heights.

In July 2008 a suicide bomb attack on an Indian Embassy in Kabul kills over fifty persons. In September that same year, President Bush sends an additional 4,500 US soldiers to Afghanistan.

In December 2009 after weeks of procrastination on the subject US President Barack Obama sends an additional 30,000 US soldiers to Afghanistan. An Al-Qaeda double agent kills seven CIA agents in a suicide attack on a US base in Khost.

May 2011 after the death of Osama bin Laden, many high profile Afghan officials were assassinated in retribution to bin Laden's death. In October the same year, as relations with Pakistan worsen, Afghanistan and India sign a partnership to expand their mutual cooperation with security and development.

June 2011 hundreds of armed Kuchi nomads supported by Taliban attacked a district in Ghazni Province looting and burning twenty six villages and killing five people. The Kuchi ambushed them at night, blew up a mobile phone tower, and blocked roads.

In 2012 at the writing of this book, Taliban resurgences continue to cause unrest by periodic attacks. United States troops continue a peace keeping role, but tensions in Afghanistan remain high and the American troops are to be withdrawn.

REFERENCES

DECLASSIFIED WHITE HOUSE MEMORANDUM

The following document is a discussion of events between President Ford and Secretary of State Henry Kissinger concerning Lebanon after the murder of the American Ambassador Francis Meloy, and evacuation of American Citizens.

MEMORANDUM

THE WHITE HOUSE
WASHINGTON

~~SECRET~~/NODIS/XGDS

DECLASSIFIED • E.O. 12353 Sec. 3.6
~~WITH PORTIONS EXEMPTED~~
~~E.O. 12053 Sec. 1.5( )~~

MEMORANDUM OF CONVERSATION

RR 00-A7, #63; St. dept ltr 12/18/01
By _dal_ , NARA, Date _2/13/02_

PARTICIPANTS: President Ford
                   The Cabinet

DATE AND TIME: Friday, June 18, 1976
                   11:00 a.m.

PLACE: The Cabinet Room

President: Ron just announced we are evacuating Americans from Lebanon. We will leave essential people in the Embassy to keep operations going. We began announcements on VOA and BBC because communications in Beirut are so poor. There are about 1400 people in Lebanon but we have no idea how many will want to leave, because it is voluntary. Henry, why don't you describe the situation in Lebanon?

Kissinger: First, the situation about the Meloy killing. He was on his way to meet with the new President Sarkis, to discuss the situation and possible U.S. evacuation.

[He describes the assassination.]

To the best of our information, the killing was done by a splinter group of the rejectionist front. To our best knowledge, it was done without PLO involvement. All the Arabs have condemned the act, unlike the Sudan killings.

We will evacuate tomorrow. We will not announce the route. We have been given adequate assurances and most of the route is through Syrian-held territory. We have made adequate contingency preparations but it is important not to comment on this.

We don't know how many will leave. Many have no other real home, but there is no security in Beirut. But none of the responsible groups has any real interest in killing Americans, because if there was, it could be done quite easily at any time. But there are, of course,

~~SECRET~~/NODIS/XGDS

CLASSIFIED BY   BRENT SCOWCROFT
EXEMPT FROM GENERAL DECLASSIFICATION
SCHEDULE OF EXECUTIVE ORDER 11652
EXEMPTION CATEGORY   5 (b) (1, 3)
AUTOMATICALLY DECLASSIFIED ON   Imp. to det.

PAGE ONE

Source: *Gerald Ford Presidential Library Archives*

totally irresponsible elements. But the overall situation in Lebanon is developing in a way that is not unhelpful to our interests. Lebanon is a tragedy. In U.S. equivalents, four million people have been killed.

In March, the Syrians said they were moving in in 48 hours. The Israelis said they would move in that case. If that happened, we would have united all the Arabs against it. If Israel didn't act and if Syria cleaned it up, we would be accused by Egypt of colluding with the Syrians. But if the Syrians didn't move, the radicals could dominate Lebanon and Syria would then be squeezed between a radical Lebanon and Iraq.

We maneuvered our way through this and governmental changes were made. [He describes the election, etc.] But there was no security so the political changes couldn't take place. So Syria decided to act. [Describes Syrian-held territory.]

It looks now like no one will gain an overwhelming victory. What is likely to emerge is an Arab solution with no one in predominance, with the PLO weakened, but with Egypt relatively content and Syria as well. The end result should be a strategic situation which is favorable to us, because Syria and Egypt probably will get back together. We must remember that we are the only ones who are really in touch with all the parties and the only useful force working with all of them. [Compares with the Soviets] It could blow up, of course, but if it goes on track, that is a likely outcome.

A spectacular Syrian defeat probably would overthrow Assad. With this probable moderate outcome, we are in a good position for peace. If we can keep all the radicals from uniting, or all the Arabs, it looks like a positive aspect to the tragedy of Lebanon.

Secretary Richardson: Why did the Syrians support the Christians and what kept them from a spectacular victory?

Kissinger: The Christians were about to be wiped out and that would have given Lebanon to the radicals who would have squeezed the Syrians. A spectacular Syrian victory in March could have given them a need to prove their Arab nature and turn on the Christians; this would have radicalized Jordan and put pressure on the Saudis and isolated Egypt. They didn't win spectacularly, first because it is an agony for them to be attacking the PLO, and second they underestimated the strength they faced.

[The next item was a campaign update.]

[The next item was our line on busing.]

PAGE TWO

138

A PERSONAL ACCOUNT OF THE CIVIL WAR IN LEBANON

The following account is written by the sister of Rachel, secretary to Dr. Charles Simkins and the United Nations FOA project in Lebanon, and who has been mentioned throughout this book.

I am writing down these memories of our last months in war torn Lebanon so that our children will have a record of what we lived through. We were marvelously lucky to escape. I must add that we were often quite careless. The truth is we did not fully realize it was really war. In May 1975 a major part of *Hadeth*, a suburb of Beirut, had been destroyed but a lull in the fighting followed and people were starting to clean up. We had seen the devastation on our trips to the mountains, but as nothing had happened in our part of town, we stayed home.

We lived in a comfortable old house which belonged to my husband's family and where he and his siblings were born. We enjoyed its renovation, but kept as much as possible of its traditional character, including its original hard carved wooden doors. The one story house was shaped like a horseshoe and made out of one foot square blocks of mud brick, covered with cement and then plastered over. This made it suitable for the Beirut climate. In front of the house was a large paved court yard which was always full of plants, customary in Lebanon. This was enclosed by a six foot high curved wall. A wooden door opened into a narrow street.

Our location was excellent. A few minutes' walk from the beautiful Saint Georges Bay, with its harbor always filled with pleasure boats, and the Saint Georges' Hotel. We were near *Hamra* Street, the Fifth Avenue of Beirut lined with luxury shops, cafes, and cinemas. Nearest to us was the newer Holiday Inn, and almost equidistant in the opposite direction the Murr Tower (at the time under construction) visible from our courtyard. This became an ideal location during the civil war, with gunman perched on its top, and returned gunfire which came from the top floors of the Holiday Inn. Our home was caught in between, and we never knew when a rocket aimed at either structure would fall short and hit our home.

During the summer of 1975 there were sporadic clashes in Beirut suburbs and in other parts of the country, with lulls occurring every other day. The downtown area of Beirut received the most shelling, but no one expected the Hamra area and the extensive hotel district to be attacked.

In September 1975 we visited a close Palestinian friend whose husband had been killed by a bomb while he was driving in his car. The family lived in *Nabaa* an eastern suburb which had been the center of fierce fighting for weeks. Turning the last corner before her house we were abruptly stopped by a Palestinian checkpoint. It was too late to turn back they would have shot at us. We had to think fast. I was dressed in black for such a sad visit. Black is a color worn by many Arab women, I quickly covered my face with my handkerchief to hide my face and my foreign features. They let us through. At the house the bereaved widow begged us to leave immediately for our safety. She wondered how we were even allowed through.

From her windows she saw cars everyday being pulled over, drivers forced to show their identifications, and since this was a Muslim roadblock, any Christians were dragged away to a nearby mosque, tortured and killed and their bodies thrown outside. While we were visiting, one of our friends' sons checked on the roadblock and found the gunman had gone so we left immediately.

On October 9, 1975 a young *Kataeb*, a member of one of the Christian militias, came to our house and asked to use the phone. The Moslems had surprise attacked the block of houses at the end of the narrow street behind our house. There had been no gunshots and two families had barricaded themselves in their homes. Half an hour later a dozen Kataebs silently came down the alley to our house. They were all young, pale, tired, and frightened. We let them in and some crept cautiously to the back of the houses which were under attack to help people out of

140

windows. They escorted them swiftly through our back door and out our front to the Saint Vincent de Paul School. In Lebanese style we offered all who came through coffee, lemonade, and fruit but they refused telling us that we would need all our food and drink.

Our car was parked in the alley near the kitchen wall with my eleven year old standing between the wall and the car. Just then a rocket streaked over our house and buried itself in the ground a short distance on the other side of our car. Rubble riddled our car, smashed the two side windows and ruptured all four tires. Miraculously my child was not injured, but too frightened to move. A Kataeb quickly carried him to the courtyard. We then hurried with the other families to the school.

We spent the night huddled together against a wall in a classroom, nervous, unsettled, worried, and unable to sleep because of the shelling and explosions. Through the windows of the school we could see rockets streaking across from one side of the row of windows to the other, and steady streams of tracer bullets. Every two hours our maid, who knew all our neighbors came bravely to give us updates on the events taking place.

The next day the Christian militiamen let two families leave to check on others forced to stay behind. One woman had hidden her husband in a small hen house in their back yard. If he had been caught he would have been immediately killed. When all the Christians in our area had been evacuated, the Kataebs pulled back to the Holiday Inn and the civilians remained at the school where we were brought for safety.

The following evening two elderly neighbors asked if my family would stay with them overnight. A small candle was placed in the courtyard for us. We closed the heavy door so my children could dress for bed. Just then a blinding light and deafening sound of a bomb exploding shattered the lower portion of the door. I opened the door to a shower of bullets surrounding the house. I yelled out my husband's name, and the Kataebs heard the Christian name and stopped shooting. They did not know that we there. We were rushed back to the school and remained there for fifteen days.

Thirty seven persons were at the school. We remained under continuous heavy fire. During the first few days, even tanks did not want to brave the shelling to bring us bread. One day a house across the street was hit by a rocket and caught on fire. A man came running out and was shot. He lay on the street the whole night, we could hear him moaning. The sisters at the school wanted to help the man but when they opened the front door of the school, the street was sprayed with gunfire. An army tank tried to rescue him but had to retreat because of heavy shelling. The fate of the injured man was never known.

Another day the sisters were visited by another fighting faction. They proudly showed the sister's pouches of human ears cut from their victims as proof of their kills. Thank God they respected the school. As the war intensified, there were more cases of torture, mutilation, and random killing of innocent civilians. All sides involved needed to share the guilt.

On the thirteen day a truce was agreed upon. We returned to our street and found that every house except ours had been looted. It was only saved because of the guns in plain sight of the Kataebs just across the boulevard. They had used our house for shelter and to pass through to stay out of the sight of snipers. When they left they locked all the windows and doors. They had even covered our television set and moved all our furniture to one side so as to protect it as they ran through the house. Otherwise nothing had been disturbed.

We packed all we could in our delivery truck and with our children and maid drove to the mountains for safety. We went to the home of one of our employees. The mountain area was predominantly Christian and felt they would remain safe regardless of what would happen in Beirut. My husband and I spend the night back at the school. The silence that night was eerie after all the continuous noise of fighting the previous thirteen nights.

The next day we went to Baalbek, about fifty miles northeast of Beirut to remove the furniture from my sisters apartment. We were accompanied by a Christian *Moukhtar* (a town manager), and a Moslem policeman thinking the balance would be safer. She had been evacuated to Damascus after threats were made on her life. She was the only foreigner living in a predominantly Moslem village which was very near to a Palestinian camp. My sister Rachel had come with two United Nations employees to help her move. We had to work fast. Rachel had to return to Damascus, and we had to go to *Chtaura* an hour's drive, all before dark to avoid snipers and bandits.

In our haste I did not ask Rachel for a cashier's check which my father had given on her recent trip home. He knew conditions were unstable and wanted me to have money in case of necessity. We could have cashed it on the Christian side, our bank was in the Moslem sector and there was no communication between the two. No bank would cash a check written on a bank in the opposite sector. Fate was that if we had gotten the check that day we may have spent the money and not had enough to eventually leave the country.

We stayed in *Broummana* the mountain village for twenty four days where our employee lived. There was news that a "peace treaty" had been agreed on and schools would open on the following Monday, December 8, 1975. We drove back to our home in Beirut with all our belongings on Friday, December 5th and spent the day cleaning our house. That afternoon my husband and I took a walk around our neighborhood for several streets behind our house. We found that no one had returned and that the houses had all been looted and burned.

From a distance they looked untouched, but upon closer inspection we could see the walls were pockmarked by bullet holes and shrapnel, and through the damaged doors and windows we saw the blackened ruins of the interiors. It was an unnatural stillness that night and we decided to return to the safety of the mountains the next day. No one would travel before 9:00 AM which seemed to be the time the snipers went off duty, and barricades that materialized unexpectedly in the dark had been dismantled by then.

But Saturday morning at 9:30 AM, the radio announced a massacre had taken place in the downtown area. A couple of days before the ceasefire, a Christian man who had two sons, the older a lawyer and the younger studying to be a doctor; his lawyer son had been brutally killed. His son's corpse had been mutilated and was exposed for everyone to see. The mourning father then learned his younger son had been kidnapped and killed in spite of the ceasefire. Enraged, he and his relatives armed with Kalashnikovs went to the Moslem sector and killed over a hundred people. The actual number may have been exaggerated, but in no time metal shutters clanged down on store fronts and heavily manned barricades appeared everywhere, effectively cutting Beirut off from the rest of Lebanon. No one could enter or leave the city, to try meant certain death.

We were stuck in our alley with a few other families who had also returned because of the ceasefire. We spent the rest of Saturday and Sunday keeping our children occupied and trying to divert their attention. We visited immediate neighbors and listened with anxiety to radio reports of outbreaks of violence in other areas of the city as well as in different parts of the country. Hostilities were spreading. We couldn't even cross the boulevard in front of our house as the leftists in the Murr Tower and the rightists in the Holiday Inn were firing steadily at each other and we would be caught in the cross fire.

On Monday, December 8th I told everyone to get ready for lunch. I sat in the living room fixing a window curtain waiting for my husband and son to finish a game, when I saw men carrying guns sneaking up to our neighbor's doorway, in the narrow street behind our house. Through an open bedroom window our maid heard the men breaking down the door of the adjoining house. This would enable them to enter the alley which was our only escape route.

My husband picked up the suitcase that had changes of clothes

144

for the family. In my haste I grabbed my handbag but not my husband's passport. Our lunch was ready on the table, the maid insisted on going back to get the *tabbouleh*, a Lebanese salad that takes a long time to make. She said that she had worked too hard on it to just leave it to them. We closed the courtyard door behind her just as the gunmen appeared in the alley. We fled to the school, quietly warning everyone on the way.

This time at the school we numbered seventeen refugees and eight sisters. We stayed two nights, all the while shells exploded and scattered shrapnel all around us, rockets smashed into buildings, and the rapid fire of Kalashnikovs clattered uninterruptedly. We were sure we would not survive, but miraculously the school never received a direct hit. At noon on a Wednesday, as we were getting ready to eat, a Moslem fighter whose children were students at the school came rushing in. He told the sisters that he and his men would cover their retreat to a safer place. The sisters said they would leave only if the seventeen people they were sheltering were also allowed to leave with them. Two by two we all ran across the street as fast as we could, while the Moslems kept up a steady fire in all directions to cover our escape. The Kataebs must have seen the sisters' habits and the civilians because not one shot answered the volley of fire.

I asked the Lebanese Moslem leader to let me go to my home to get some clothes. We only had what we were wearing. Our maid and a sister offered to go with me and a soldier was ordered to accompany us. He led us on a roundabout route to the back door of our house, and as we turned the last corner a man emerged from a burned house, picking his teeth as if he had just eaten. He was a *Saïka* commando, the Syrian backed PLO organization, well trained and tough. His hand went automatically for his gun, which fortunately was not there. Our escort quickly explained who we were, where we were going, and what we wanted. All the time the Saïka was talking, he motioned us to go forward.

We hurried to the house and found all the doors smashed and open, seven bare bed frames, all our books piled in the middle of the living room, as a bonfire ready to be lit. All the closets were empty with a few pieces of clothing scattered about. None of my husband's clothes remained. The kitchen had also been looted so totally, that not even a toothpick was left.

I grabbed a sheet that was crumbled on the floor, and piled everything in it I could find. The bathroom was the only room untouched; I took towels, toothbrushes, and combs. I also salvaged the children's photo albums which had been thrown on the pile of books. I was so heartsick and stunned that my movements were slowed and indecisive. Our escort was frightened and he urged me continually to hurry. He was unarmed as the sisters had insisted he leave his gun behind, thinking he would be safer without it. I told him not to worry because the commandos were his allies. "Oh no" he replied, "The Saïka are not with us. There are many factions under the PLO umbrella, and they are not all friends and allies."

I gathered what I could and we hurried out following our escort, who returned by a circuitous route to avoid any Saïka guerrillas. When we came to a high wall I could not climb over, he shoved me over it while a PLO gunman aimed his rifle at me ready to shoot. Leaving our escort to explain our presence – he claimed that we were under the protection of the top PLO leader in that sector – we ran. Our saviors sent us at full speed to the Salesian School Rue Verdun, where my husband was anxiously waiting for us.

The school was our refuge for the next thirty three days. My family was given a classroom and the other refugees divided according their choice. The Salesian School was Catholic but its students were mostly Moslem children who lived in the neighborhood. These children would play in the school yard, and my boys would join them.

Our good Samaritans this time were seven Salesian priests: five Italian, one Irish, and one Syrian. They did their best within their limited means to see that we had all we needed. We spent Christmas there. At midnight while rockets crashed in the distance, one of the priests sneaked three brightly wrapped packages into our classroom, gifts for our children. The gifts revealed T-shirts with Salesian School on them, tube socks, candy, and puzzles. The children were excited with these unexpected gifts. The next day the boys asked my husband and I to leave the classroom for a while. When we returned they presented us with small wooden crosses made from tree branches which were attached from the string from their gifts as pendants.

During the thirty three day stay my husband only left the school once when he and I could no longer stand the confinement, we decided to visit an old Doctor friend that lived behind the Salesian school. We could not leave from the back of the school because there was no rear exit. We were forced to leave by the front entrance and take several left turns and then down a narrow alley to his home. Our friend was pleased to see us and served traditional Arabic coffee, the first we had tasted in a month.

We left our Doctor friends' house about 3:30 in the afternoon, and crossed the street to go back to the school. We walked leisurely down the sidewalk enjoying our brief sensation of freedom. A jeepload of Saïka commandos came down the street from the opposite direction. They stared at us intently and we became terrified, and then we heard the screech of their tires as they reversed and came barreling down the street toward us. We were in the alley by this time and ran for our lives and dashed into the school. From a window we could see the commandos driving slowly by, searching in every direction. We knew it was not safe to have gone out, but after so many days, you get a feeling that it does not matter anymore. The priests advised my husband not to leave the building again, and not even show himself at a window.

Later, the priests at the school received some money from a charitable organization to help with their relief work. They opted to give needed cash to each of the refugees. What a windfall, I bought carefully and was able to buy five sweaters. We were always cold. Our maid, an older Lebanese woman, and myself walked to the seafront area where the sidewalk merchants had

147

set up their stalls after the downtown *souks* were destroyed. As we were walking back to the school, our maid noticed a jeep filled with armed Palestinians drive by slowly in the opposite direction. They were looking at me. When they turned a corner we began to run. The older lady could not run as fast, she saw the jeep coming back in our direction. She and the maid shoved me behind a wall and told me to stay there while they continued walking. The jeep passed again and the jeep only saw two Arabic women walking and talking. It sped on its way and the women called to me to hurry.

The road to the school was uphill and neither of us could run that distance. We hurried as fast as we could before the jeep returned, but were startled by an armed man who appeared directly in our path. After a heart-stopping moment, my maid began to talk and joke with the man in Arabic. She knew him from *Broummana* where he usually worked for a family we knew there. He let us pass safely.

Since our children played with the Moslem children, it was discovered that their father was also at the school. His life was in danger. With the help of the priests' driver, we could drive to get him a new passport, but we had no money and no way to cross the "No man's" area separating the Christian and Moslem sectors, and no one accepted checks. Besides all the banks were closed.

One day when everyone was downstairs in the dining room, and I was upstairs helping one of my children, the phone next to me rang. Since no one else was around, I answered it. It was the United Nations in Damascus calling the UN in Beirut. They were permitted one phone call and by error had called the school. I pleaded with the operator to leave the line open and to call my sister. Before telephone communications out of Lebanon became impossible to use, I had been able to call her. She knew we needed money desperately to buy airline tickets. Flying out of the country was our only hope. By this time I was frantic because fighting was getting much closer to the school and the priests were trying to find a hiding place for my husband. There were two other convents in the area sheltering Christian refugees. Saïka commandos had already invaded them and beaten the adult males. One was so badly hurt he was not expected to live.

Meanwhile my sister was begging the American Embassy in Damascus to help, but they could do nothing. The border between Lebanon and Syria was closed. Father Leary, the Irish priest, offered a solution. He had a friend in the Irish contingent of the UN peacekeeping force (the "Blue Berets") in Beirut, a Major Murphy. This contingent supervised the border between southern Lebanon and Israel. Major Murphy in turn, had a UN friend stationed in Damascus, Major Callaghan. Murphy telexed Callaghan using the direct UN line, to visit my sister in Damascus, and tell her from me that time was running out for us to get money to leave the country.

Murphy then went to Jerusalem to spend Christmas with his family before returning to Beirut to close up the UN office there. Callaghan was invited to join them for the holidays. Callaghan visited my sister Rachel at her office and told her that he would be leaving the following day for Jerusalem. With the help of a Syrian friend Rachel was able to cash the cahier check for US dollars and Lebanese pounds. The official Syrian policy was to give Syrian pounds only, a nonconvertible currency, unless special permission could be given to receive foreign currency.

Rachel gave this money to Callaghan to take to Murphy, knowing it was a gamble because UN soldiers driving up from Israel to Beirut were often robbed; even UN vehicles were taken. We were lucky Murphy delivered the money to Father Leary who handed it to us the day after Christmas. But it was not enough money for five tickets, so we began to worry and contemplate our options again.

We learned that the *Lycee Francais*, which had a kindergarten in the neighborhood, was going to open at the beginning of the New Year. The previous June, I had enrolled my children and paid for the first quarter, more than one thousand Lebanese Pounds. I decided to ask for a refund. The supervisor of the Lycee had just returned from France. I told her about our predicament and asked if we could get back at least part of our payment. She gave me the whole amount. It was the same amount of cash that she had left. She showed me the empty envelope.

During these stressful days we also had to obtain an American visa for my husband. As long as he remained inside he was safe. My maid and I walked to the Embassy, skirting buildings and retaining walls along the way; we expected to be shot by snipers at every step. We entered the embassy grounds almost in a crouch position to keep as low a profile as possible, and were almost shot by a US Marine on guard. That was the day the Vice Consul could not reach the Consulate even by tank. Only five employees were in the building.

The arguments began. The Consular employee refused to give a visa to my husband. He said that my children and I could leave and my husband could follow later -- "If he were still alive," I added. There was shouting in Arabic, French, and English, a typically Arabic scene before the visa was granted. But my maid and I had to return the next day to get the passport. Perhaps the Consul person thought that my husband would not make it.

On a Thursday I called the American Embassy to enquire about transportation and they sent a man to sell us plane tickets. I did not trust the man. He was Palestinian and evasive in his answers to me. He said we would have to make our own way to the airport. Also, that the plane was not leaving until Saturday, and the Priests were told by Moslem friends that within a day or two, the school would be searched for Christian men. We did not dare to wait until Saturday. I phoned Air France and the clerk told me if we could get to a nearby hotel, he would guarantee our safe passage to the airport. And a plane was leaving the next day.

On Friday morning we left for the hotel in a taxi driven by a Moslem known to the Salesians. We thanked the priests for all their help and received their blessings. We arrived at the designated hotel moments later and transferred to a large Mercedes painted gray with the word "MAIL" on its sides in bright yellow, in English and Arabic. It was the car that brought mail to Air France at the airport. My husband sat between the Greek Orthodox driver and a Moslem. I was in back with the children. We were warned not to talk and not to look frightened if we were stopped.

The airport was already in view when several gunmen stepped onto the road and stopped us, guns all pointing at the car. We tried to look calm and unconcerned, but my heart pounded and I was terrified, especially for my husband. He was in greater danger than was a woman with three young children. The driver chatted amiably with the men, and gave them some money. They lowered their guns and waved us on.

The airport was not yet badly damaged but there was no food or running water and the floor was covered with filth. Corridors had been used as lavatories. But there was an enterprising Lebanese person selling souvenirs! Lebanese soldiers were everywhere. They appeared tense and nervous, showing the strain of being caught in the middle of a civil war, in a country which no longer had a viable government. The army was as divided as the country.

We boarded the Air France plane at noon and it took off almost immediately. Half and hour later the airport was attacked and badly damaged, and forced to close. Our flight was the last to leave the airport for the next twelve days.

Looking back on our life in Lebanon, we try to dwell only on the good times we had, but the nightmares are still there. We are very saddened to see the pictures of the looted and burned home we once shared as a family. We think of our neighbors often and hope they were all able to survive. The photos, taken by my sister Rachel before she left Lebanon, already showed the reclaim of nature. She told us that grass and wildflowers were already growing in the ruins of our home.

151

DEFINITIONS

I have included the following definitions of terms for the benefit and understanding of the reader. Farsi terms have been noted in brackets.

AD / BC Latin for Anno Domini which means "year after death" to delineate between history using the birth of the Christian Christ as **BC** "Before Christ" and **AD** "After Death" [of Christ]." It became a practice with religious scholars and carried over into academia and then into common use. **BCE** stands for Before the Common Era (or Current Era, or Christian Era), and **CE** for the Common Era.

AFGHAN CIVIL WAR Began after the Russians left 1996 to 2001 civil war.

AMERICAN UNIVERSITY OF BERUIT (AUB) Graduated its first class of sixteen students in December 1866. The Faculty of Agriculture opened in 1952, which became the Faculty of Agriculture and Food Sciences.

AHSEEYA [Farsi] Hand grinder.

BAIT CHAMA A small town in Lebanon near Zahl and Baalbek, Lebanon. The Simkins had a villa in Bait Chama.

BAKHSHEESH A gift or tip, something you give voluntarily and do not expect anything in return; as opposed to Reshwat, a bribe.

BAKLAVA A sweet dessert common to the Middle East area.

BOUTAH [Farsi] Generic name for a small bush.

CHASHMA [Farsi] Water spring (natural water source).

CIA Central Intelligence Agency.

CINI [also **SINI**] Chinese.

DEA Drug Enforcement Agency.

DRUZE A religion begun in 1017 AD in Cairo, Egypt. Predominantly in Israel, Syria, Lebanon, and Jordan. It is a blend of elements from Judaism, Christianity, and Islam. They believe that by having a daily direct connection to God that other rituals are therefore not necessary. They call themselves *muwahhidun*, monotheists. Their religion is closed to outsiders.

DURAND LINE A treaty established in 1893 between the British and the Afghan ruler Amir Abdur Rehman Khan. The treaty was to be enforced for 100 years.

FAO Food and Agriculture Organization of the United Nations.

GENGHIS KHAN 1165 to August 18, 1227. Mongolian warrior who united the nomadic tribes to create one of the largest empires in history. Born near the border of Russia as one of several sons of a local chieftain, by 1206 had united the Mongol tribes and earned the title Great Emperor, Genghis Khan. His army with good horsemanship, archery, and surprise attack was able to build an empire. His armies were able to travel over seventy miles a day. His empire stretched from China to the Black Sea, and north into Russia. In 1215 Genghis Khan captured Beijing, China. His sons carried on his empire, one son Kublai Khan became ruler of China and started the Yuan Dynasty. Khans Empire bridged the east and the west.

GENOCIDE The deliberate destruction of a national, ethnic, racial, or religious group or culture by another group.

GREEN LINE Line of demarcation during the Lebanese Civil War (1975 to 1990). It separated Muslim factions in west Beirut from the Christian front in east Beirut. The name came from the growth of foliage that grew in the open space between the two fighting factions.

HARB War.

HARAM Forbidden, especially as forbidden by Islamic law.

HASHISH [also **HASHISHI**] A paste-like resin obtained from the stalks of the Cannabis plant. A common cash crop in many parts of the world.

IMAM An Islamic spiritual leader. One who leads Islamic worship services especially in a mosque. The term is also used for a recognized scholar or authority about Islam.

ISLAM The word Islam means submission. Therefore a true Muslim is one who surrenders himself to God. Many passages in the Christian Old Testament are prevalent in the Koran, especially the story where Abraham was willing to sacrifice his own son in submission to God's command.

KALASHNIKOV Name of the designer of the automatic rifle commonly used the world over by militias and private citizens. Referred more often in the United States as an AK 47.

KASSIR RASAK Break your head.

KHANA [Farsi] House.

KHALIPHA [Farsi] [also **KHALIFA**] Caliph, king.

LEBANESE CIVIL WAR A war predominantly between Christians and Muslims from 1975 to 1990. Lebanon was a nation where both factions as well as Palestinians had influence in the government. Palestinian refugees in Lebanon estimated at about ten percent of the country, were influenced by the *Palestinian Liberation Organization* (PLO). Tensions boiled over by the early part of 1975. Beirut was devastated in the war.

MABAL Traditional coffee grinder but also because of its rhythmic sound is used as a musical instrument.

MAHS [Farsi] Yogurt.

MASHK [Farsi] Skin, as in animal skin. **MASKE** smaller animal skin especially used to store water for traveling or to take to the fields.

MASKA [Farsi] Butter.

MASSOUD, Ahmed Shah 1953-2001 [also **MASOOD**] Known as the "Lion of Panjshir," he fought against the Russians and then the Taliban. He is honored for his heroic resistance and love of country.

MAZARI SHARIF; MAZAR-EI SHARIF City in northeast Afghanistan which means, "Tomb of the Exalted" or "Noble Shrine", because Ali, the cousin and son in-law of Muhammad is buried there.

MONGHOL [Farsi] Referring to Mongolian descent.

MUHAMMAD Born in Mecca, Mohammad lived from 570-632 AD, observing the wickedness of the people in Mecca, he began meditating days at a time in a cave at the base of Mount Hira, a few miles north of Mecca. One night Muhammad had a vision of the angel Gabriel, the messenger of God and began preaching against the sin and corruption in Mecca. After ten years with little success and growing opposition to his teachings, he traveled to Medina in 622. The city welcomed him and the first mosque was built. In 630 Muhammad led a large force of followers against Mecca, conquered it and destroyed the idols being worshipped. Muhammad wished to unite the Arab tribes under one God.

MULLAH An educated Muslim trained in religious law and doctrine, and who usually holds an official position. The Mullah conducts the Friday sermon and prayers and marriages and funerals. They teach the laws and doctrines of Islam. Mullahs also act as arbitrators for disputes, basing their resolution on Islamic law and principles.

MUSLIM An adherent of Islam, a Muslim is one who submits to god.

NHAN [Farsi] **NON** [Persian] **KHUBZ** [Arabic] Unleavened flat bread.

OPIUM POPPIE The Poppy *Papver somniferum* from which the drug opium is harvested. Known for millennia, Egyptians would chew poppy seeds to relieve pain.

PANJSHIR The Panjshir Valley is in eastern Afghanistan. The name refers to the Valley of the Five Lions (protectors) in Afghanistan near the Hindu Kush mountain range.

QARYAH [Farsi] Village.

OKAMOTO, KOZO One of the three terrorists of the Japanese Red Army terrorist organization that attacked the Tel Aviv airport May 30, 1972. Twenty six people were killed and eighty injured. Tsuyoshi Okudaira and Yasuyuki Yasuda were the other two terrorists that were killed. All three terrorists were trained in camps in Baalbek, Lebanon.

QUROOT [Farsi] Dried cuddled milk. Yogurt or buttermilk are dried into hard pebble size chunks which are easy to store for winter, and be carried to the fields.

QUZA [Farsi] A vessel usually made of clay used for yogurt, water, or liquids.

RABABA Musical instrument with one string.

RESHWAT [Farsi] expected bribe, not volunteered.

SILK ROAD A historic network of trade routes extending from China and Southeast Asia to the Middle East. It included a portion which included the historic Khyber Pass. Named after the very successful silk trade from China, it connected early civilizations.

SUNDALEE [Farsi] Generic term for table or table like structure.

TAJIKS People inhabiting Tajikistan and neighboring areas including Afghanistan. They speak a dialect closely related to Persian.

TALIBAN Radical form of Islam, came into Afghanistan during its civil war with the promise to reinstate law and order. But their form of radical Islam became intolerable.

TANDOOR A large cone shaped clay oven used for cooking and baking. A fire at its base creates high temperatures within the oven. Tandoor ovens are still in common use in Middle East and Asian countries.

TIZ Buttocks.

USAID United States Agency for International Development. Signed as an executive order in 1961 by President John F. Kennedy, under the Foreign Assistance Act of 1961. A development assistance program with the goals to provide economic, development, and humanitarian assistance around the world in support of the foreign policy goals of the United States. In 2010 the majority of the USAID budget of 2.75 billion went to Afghanistan. *http://usaid.gov.*

YABANI Japanese.

SUGGESTED SOURCES FOR ADDITIONAL INFORMATION

BOOKS

THE KITE RUNNER by Khaled Hosseini, 2003, published by Riverhead Books, 336 pages, ISBN 978-1-59448-0001.

THE HAZARA'S OF AFGHANISTAN: An Historical, Cultural, Economic And Political Study by Sayed Askar Mousavi, 1997, published by St. Martin's Press, 288 pages, ISBN 13-978-0-31217-3869.

WEBSITES

HAZARA PEOPLES

Http://hazara.net

Http://hazaranation.com

Http://www.hazarapeople.com
[Http://hazarapeople.com/hazara/hn/Afghanistan]

AFGHANISTAN

Http://www.afghanland.com

Http://www.afghanistans.com/information

Http://en.wikipedia.org/wiki/Timeline_of_Afghanistan

ABOUT THE AUTHOR

Yazdan Bakhsh was born in Afghanistan where as a child he was raised in the high mountains. As a young adult he traveled to other Middle Eastern countries to work. While working in Lebanon he met his American family. After surviving a civil war and numerous life threatening events, Yazdan was eventually able to come to the United States, a dream he never imagined.